STAR WARS™

WORKBOOKS

# FIRST PHONICS

FOR AGES 4–5

BY THE EDITORS OF BRAIN QUEST
EDUCATIONAL CONSULTANT: CHARLOTTE RABY

**SCHOLASTIC**

Scholastic Children's Books
Euston House,
24 Eversholt Street,
London NW1 1DB, UK

A division of Scholastic Ltd
London ~ New York ~ Toronto ~ Sydney ~ Auckland
Mexico City ~ New Delhi ~ Hong Kong

First published in the USA by Workman Publishing in 2014.
This edition published in the UK by Scholastic Ltd in 2016.
© & TM 2016 LUCASFILM LTD.

STAR WARS is a registered trademark of Lucasfilm Ltd.
BRAIN QUEST is a registered trademark of Workman Publishing Co., Inc., and Groupe Play Bac, S.A.

Workbook series design by Raquel Jaramillo
Cover illustration by Mike Sutfin
Interior illustrations by Mike Manley, Pat Pigott, Mark Poutenis, Eric Battle, Grant Gould, Eldon Cowgur and Scott Cohn

ISBN 978 1407 16293 5

Printed in Great Britain by Bell & Bain Ltd, Glasgow

4 6 8 10 9 7 5 3

Papers used by Scholastic Children's Books are made from woods grown in sustainable forests.

www.scholastic.co.uk

# STAR WARS

## WORKBOOKS

This workbook belongs to:

_____

# Aa

Anakin fights
an acklay
in the arena!

Copy the capital letter **A**.

Now write the capital letter **A**.

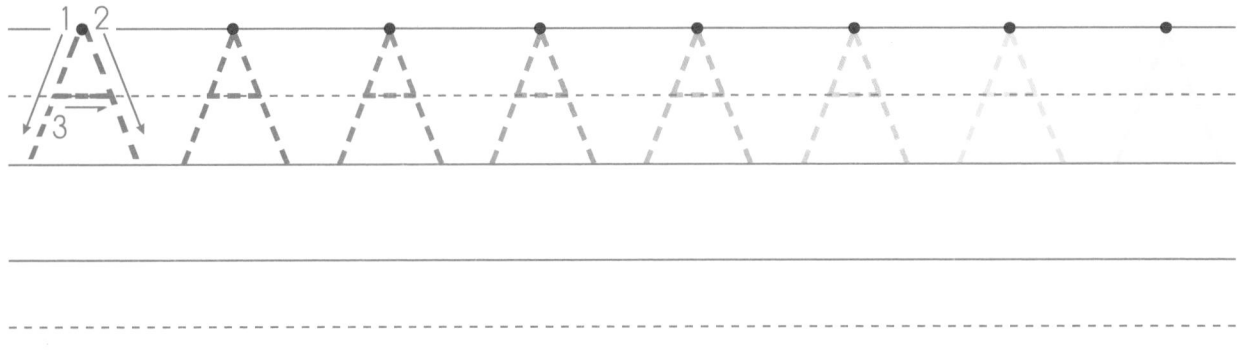

Copy the lowercase letter **a**.

Now write the lowercase letter **a**.

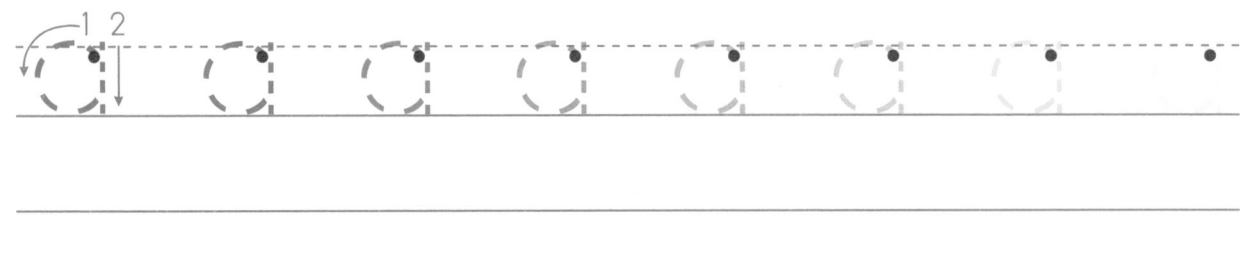

Read the words together.

Now copy the letter **A** or **a** to complete each word.

Anakin

acklay

Amidala

asteroid

Alabama

arena

# B b

Boba Fett
brings a big
bantha with him!

Copy the capital letter **B**.

Now write the capital letter **B**.

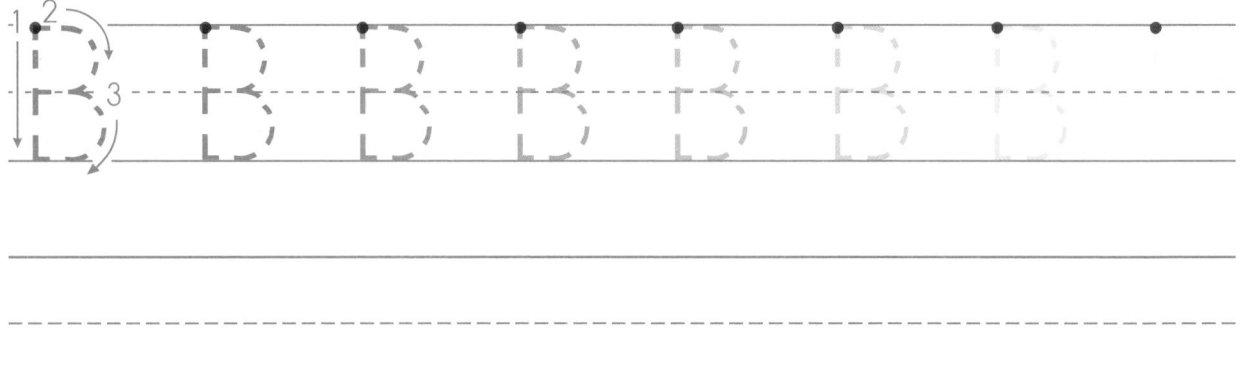

Copy the lowercase letter **b**.

Now write the lowercase letter **b**.

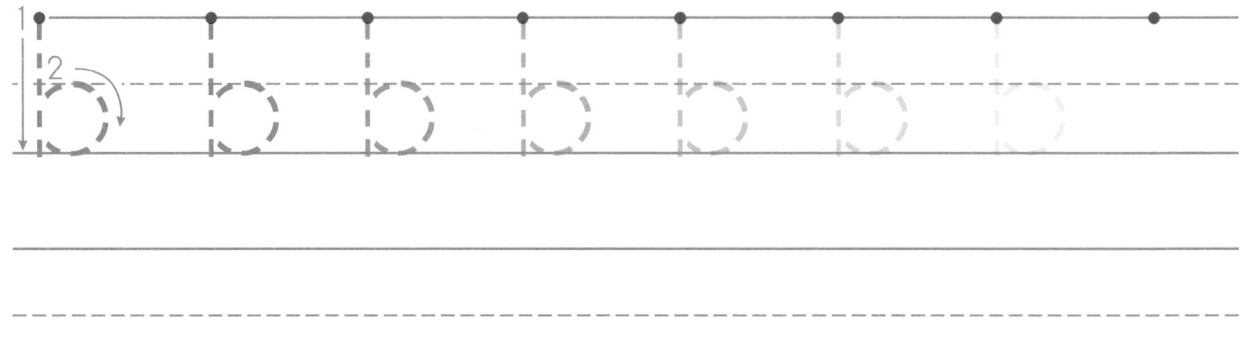

Read the words together.

Now copy the letter **B** or **b** to complete each word.

Boba      bantha

Jar Jar Binks      big

bounty      bring

# Play with A

Help **Anakin** find the **asteroid**!

Draw a line along the path with **A** and **a**.

Start

End

# Play with B

Boba Fett wants to play with a ball.

Colour the balls with **B** or **b**.

# Cc

Count Dooku counts clone troopers on the planet Coruscant.

Copy the capital letter C.

Now write the capital letter C.

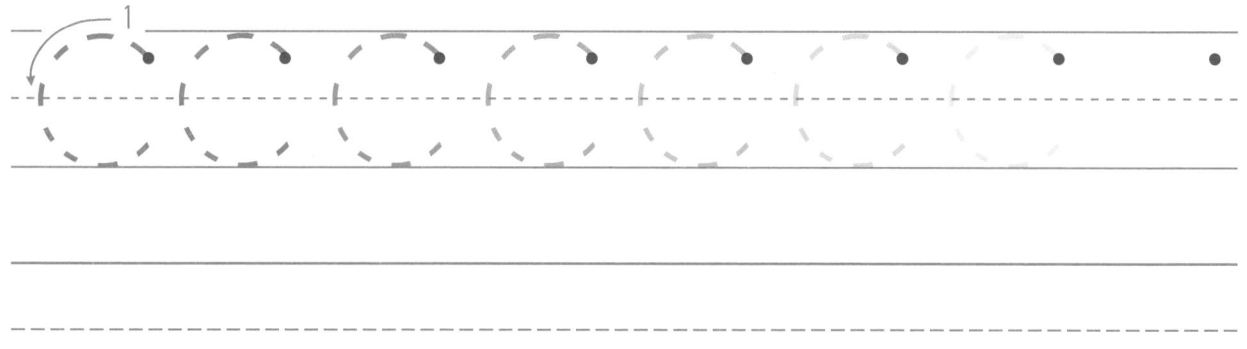

Copy the lowercase letter c.

Now write the lowercase letter c.

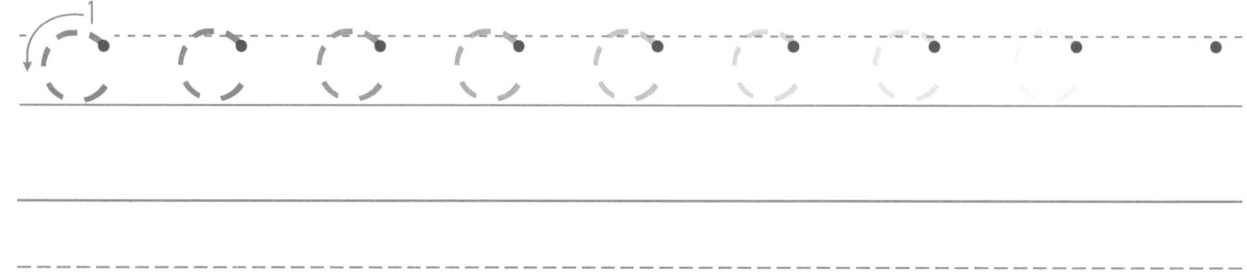

Read the words together.

Now copy the letter **C** or **c** to complete each word.

Count Dooku can

clone trooper cat

Coruscant counts

# D d

Darth Sidious draws a map for Darth Maul and the droids.

Copy the capital letter **D**.

Now write the capital letter **D**.

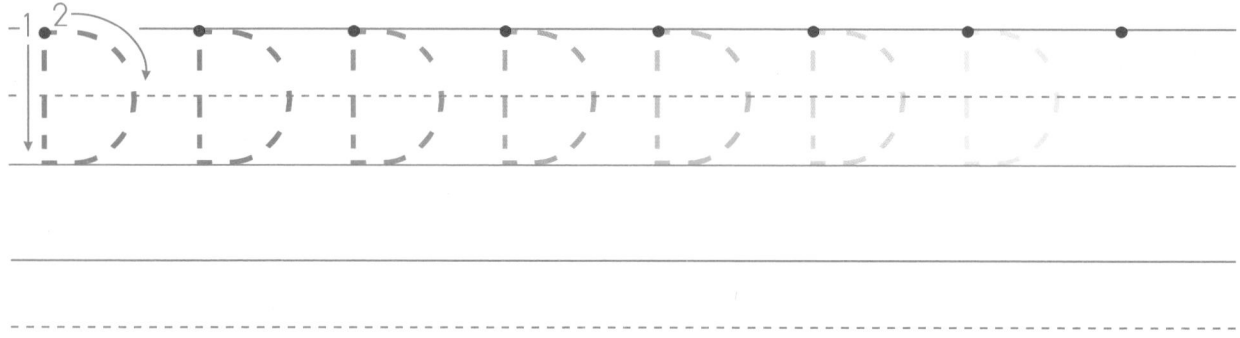

Copy the lowercase letter **d**.

Now write the lowercase letter **d**.

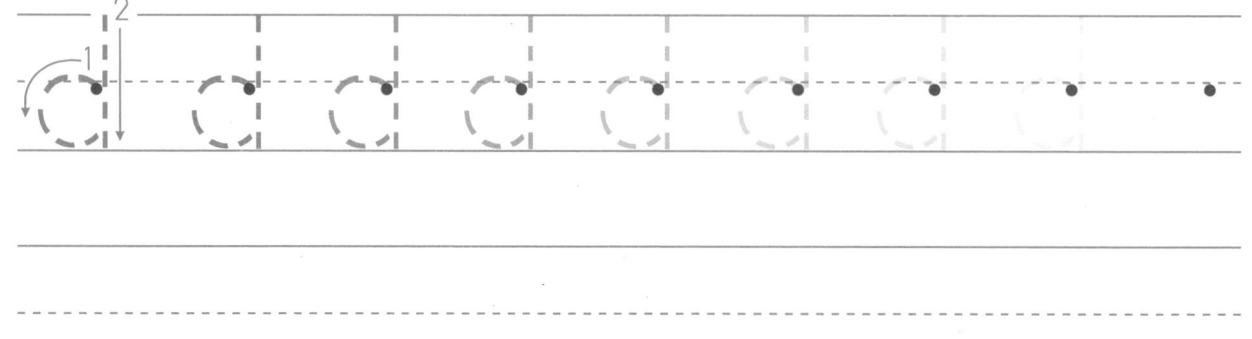

Read the words together.

Now copy the letter **D** or **d** to complete each word.

Darth Maul      draw

Dagobah      droid

Dexter      hard

# Play with C

Follow **Count** Dooku!

Draw a line along the path with **C** and **c**.

# Play with D

Welcome to the **droid** shop!

Circle the **droids** with **D** or **d**.

# Ee

The Emperor
Palpatine met
everyone on Endor.

Copy the capital letter **E**.

Now write the capital letter **E**.

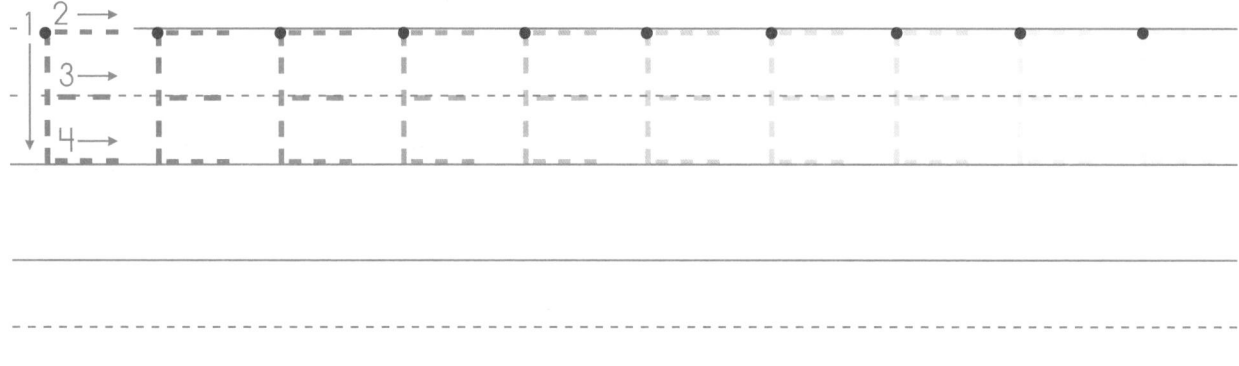

Copy the lowercase letter **e**.

Now write the lowercase letter **e**.

Read the words together.

Now copy the letter **E** or **e** to complete each word.

g⊝t　　　　⊝veryone

⊑mperor　m⊝n

⊑ndor　　m⊝t

# F f

Jango Fett likes
to fly fast!

Copy the capital letter **F**.

Now write the capital letter **F**.

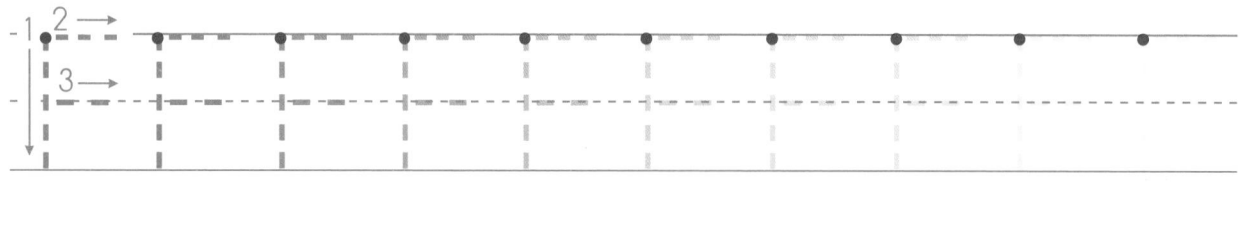

Copy the lowercase letter **f**.

Now write the lowercase letter **f**.

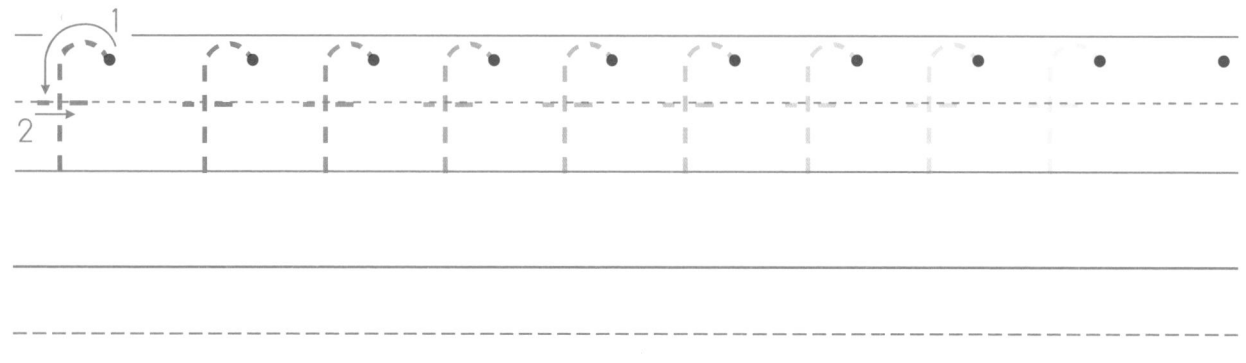

Read the words together.

Now copy the letter **F** or **f** to complete each word.

Jango Fett    fly

Kit Fisto    fast

the Force    fun

# Play with E

Help the **Ewoks** escape from **Emperor** Palpatine!

Draw a line along the path with **E** and **e**.

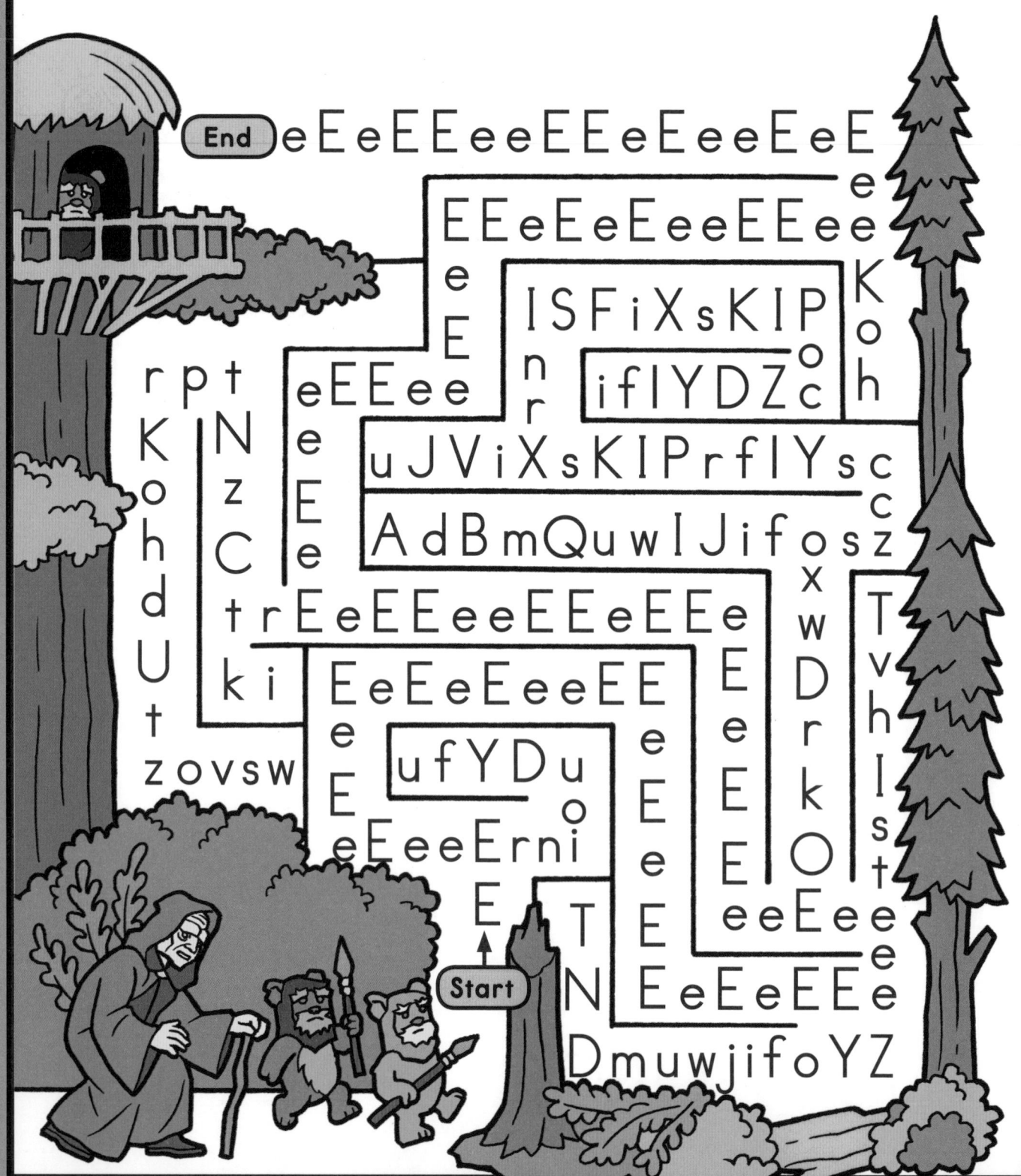

End

Start

# Play with F

Colour the spaces with **F** in green.

Colour the spaces with **f** in red.

Who do you see?

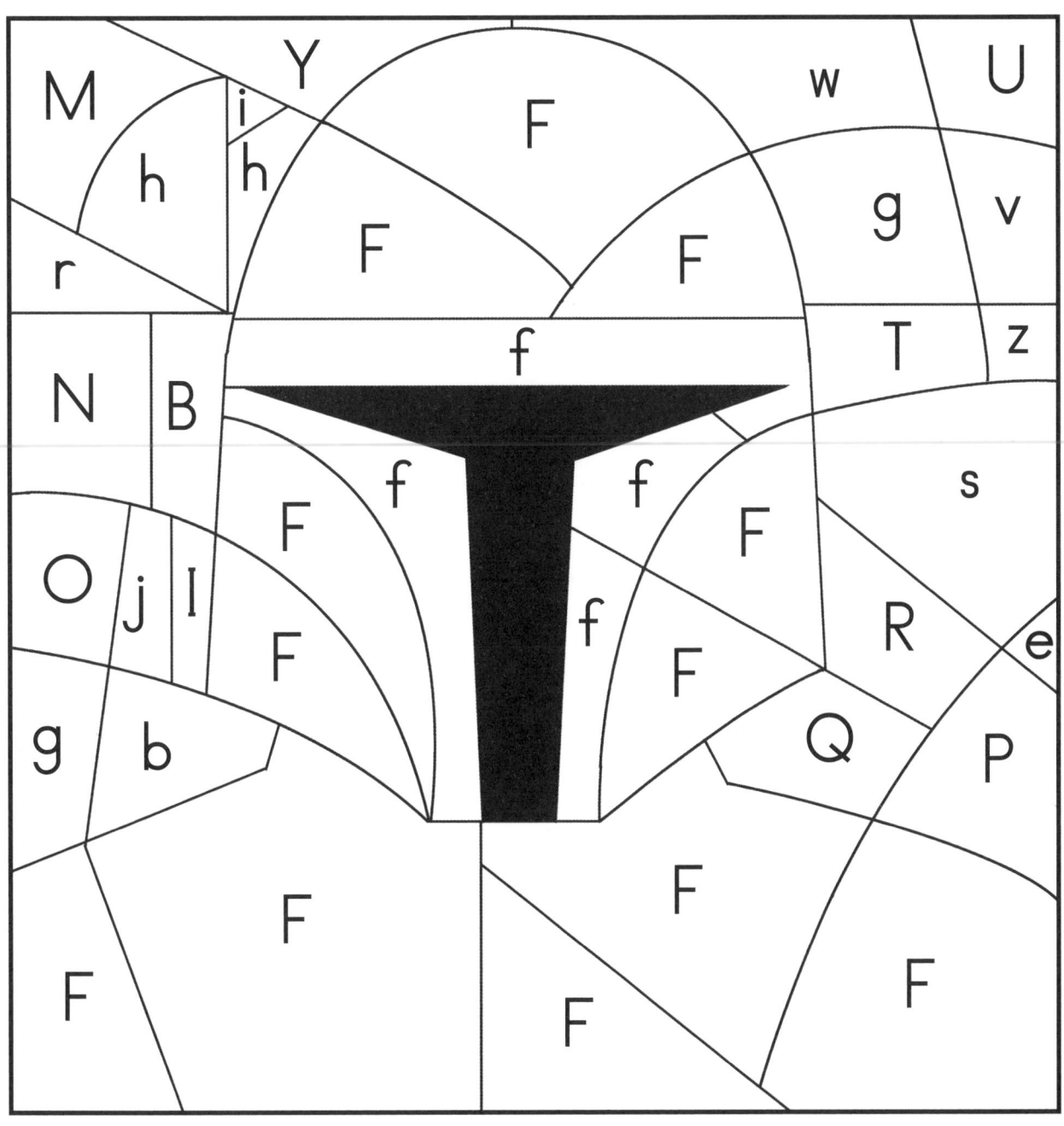

# Gg

The Gungans give up their weapons in Galactic City.

Copy the capital letter **G**.

Now write the capital letter **G**.

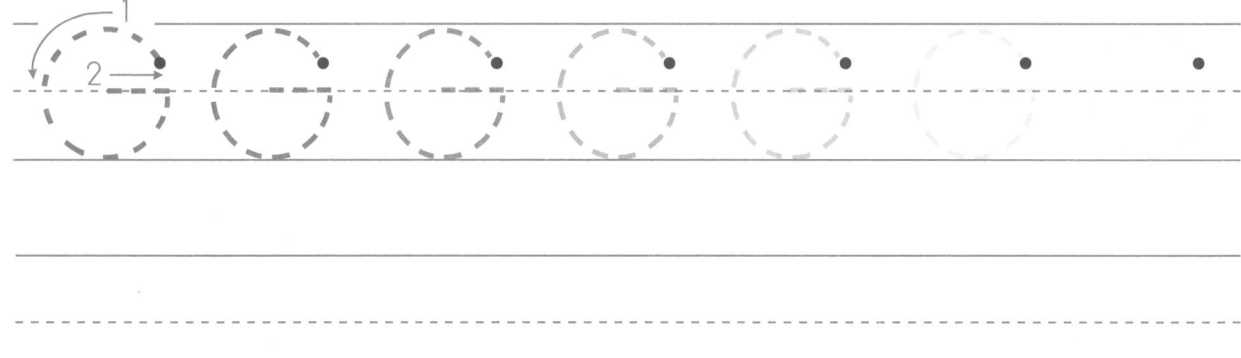

Copy the lowercase letter **g**.

Now write the lowercase letter **g**.

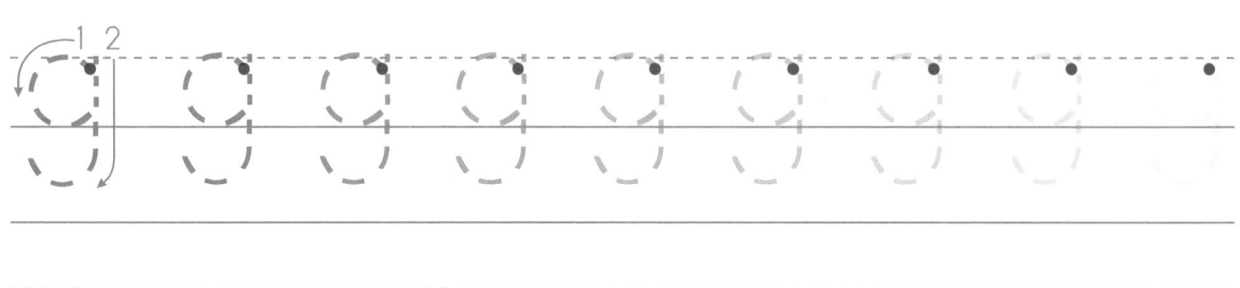

Read the words together.

Now copy the letter **G** or **g** to complete each word.

Gungan                  give

Galactic                galaxy

Grim                    song

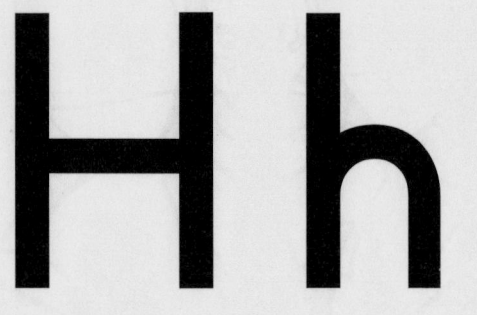

# Hh

Han Solo hides from Jabba the Hutt!

Copy the capital letter **H**.

Now write the capital letter **H**.

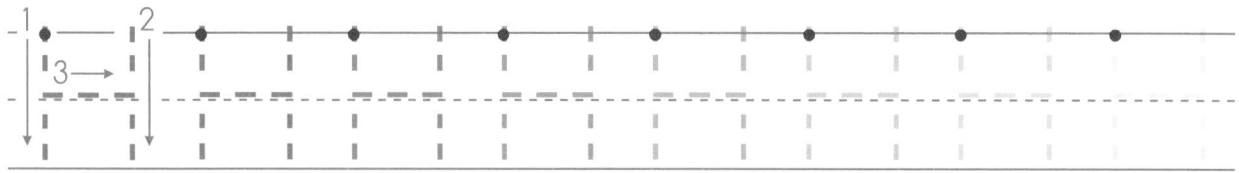

Copy the lowercase letter **h**.

Now write the lowercase letter **h**.

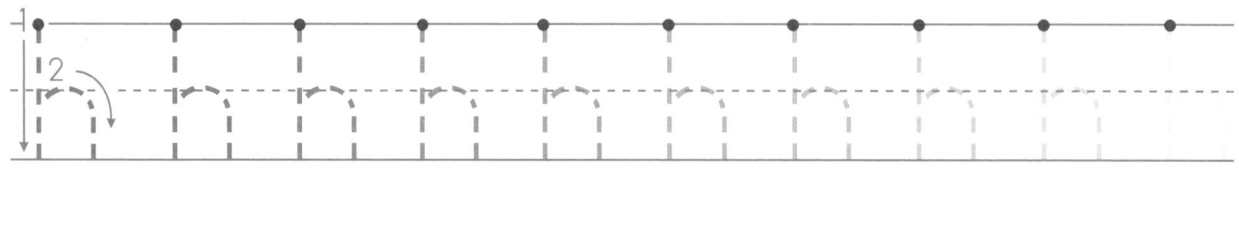

Read the words together.

Now copy the letter **H** or **h** to complete each word.

Han Solo    Hoth

Jabba the Hutt

hide    hat    have

# Play with G

Colour the spaces with **G** in grey.

Colour the spaces with **g** in blue.

Who do you see?

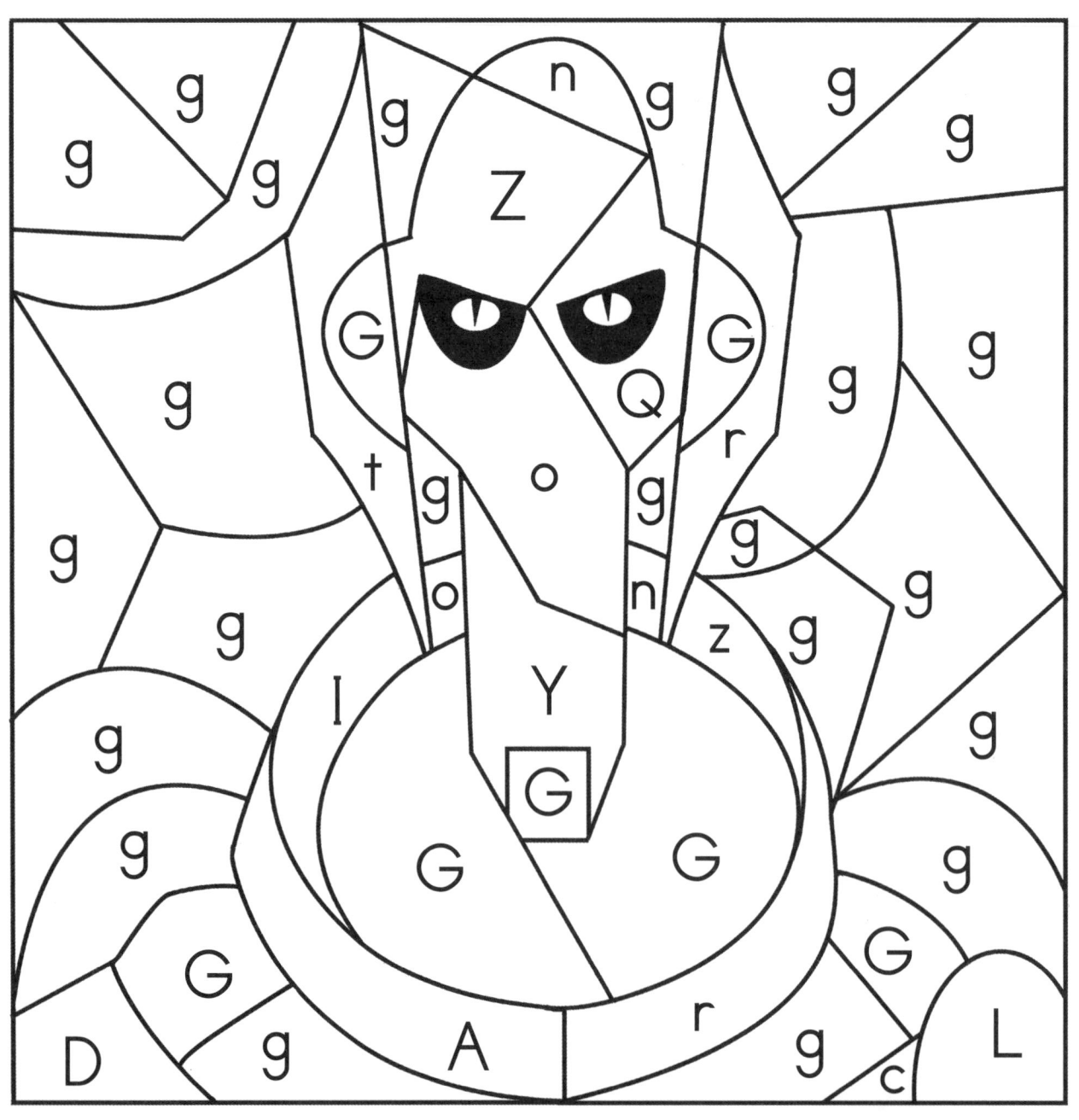

# Play with H

Help **Han** Solo through the maze to escape from the **Hutts**.

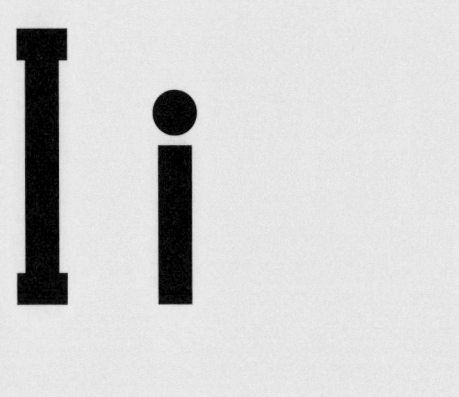

# I i

An Ithorian rides in an Imperial landspeeder.

Copy the capital letter **I**.

Now write the capital letter **I**.

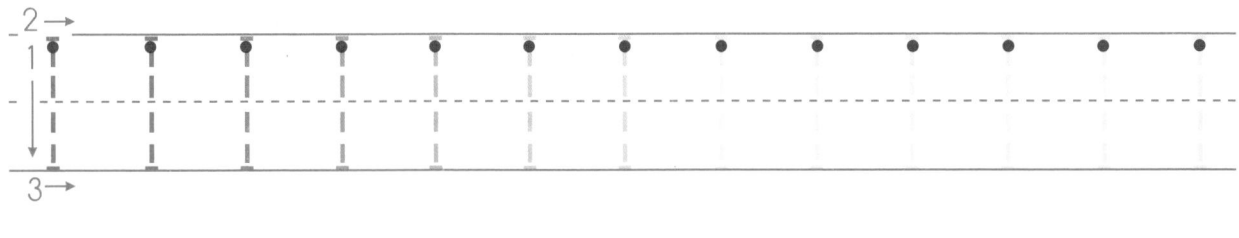

Copy the lowercase letter **i**.

Now write the lowercase letter **i**.

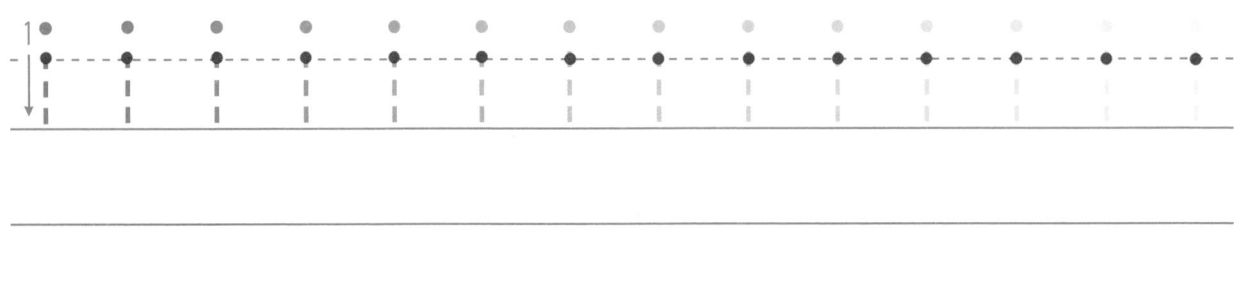

Read the words together.

Now copy the letter **I** or **i** to complete each word.

Imperial    think

Ithorian    interesting

Intergalactic    is

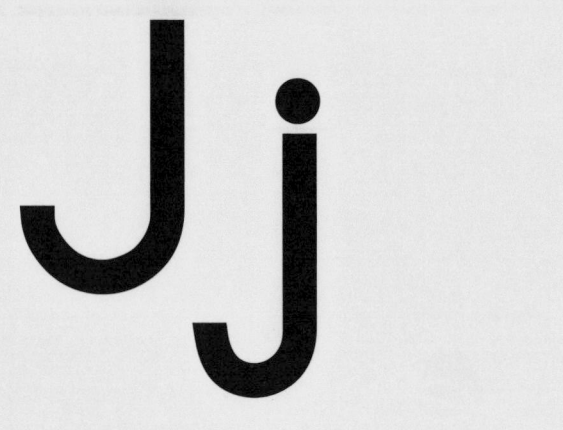

# Jj

Jar Jar tells a
joke to a Jedi.

Copy the capital letter **J**.

Now write the capital letter **J**.

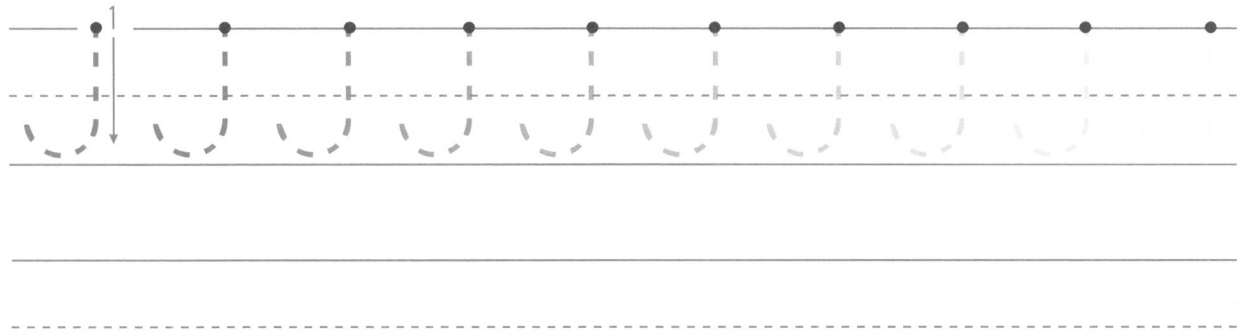

Copy the lowercase letter **j**.

Now write the lowercase letter **j**.

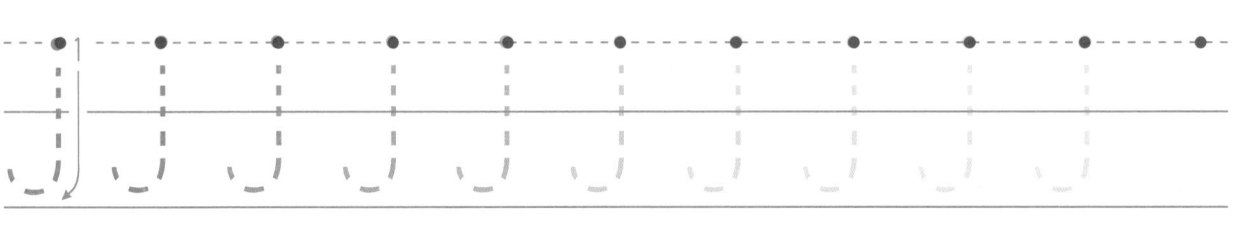

Read the words together.

Now copy the letter J or j to complete each word.

Jar Jar          join

Jedi             joke

Jabba            major

# Play with I

Colour the spaces with **I** and **i** in red.

Who do you see?

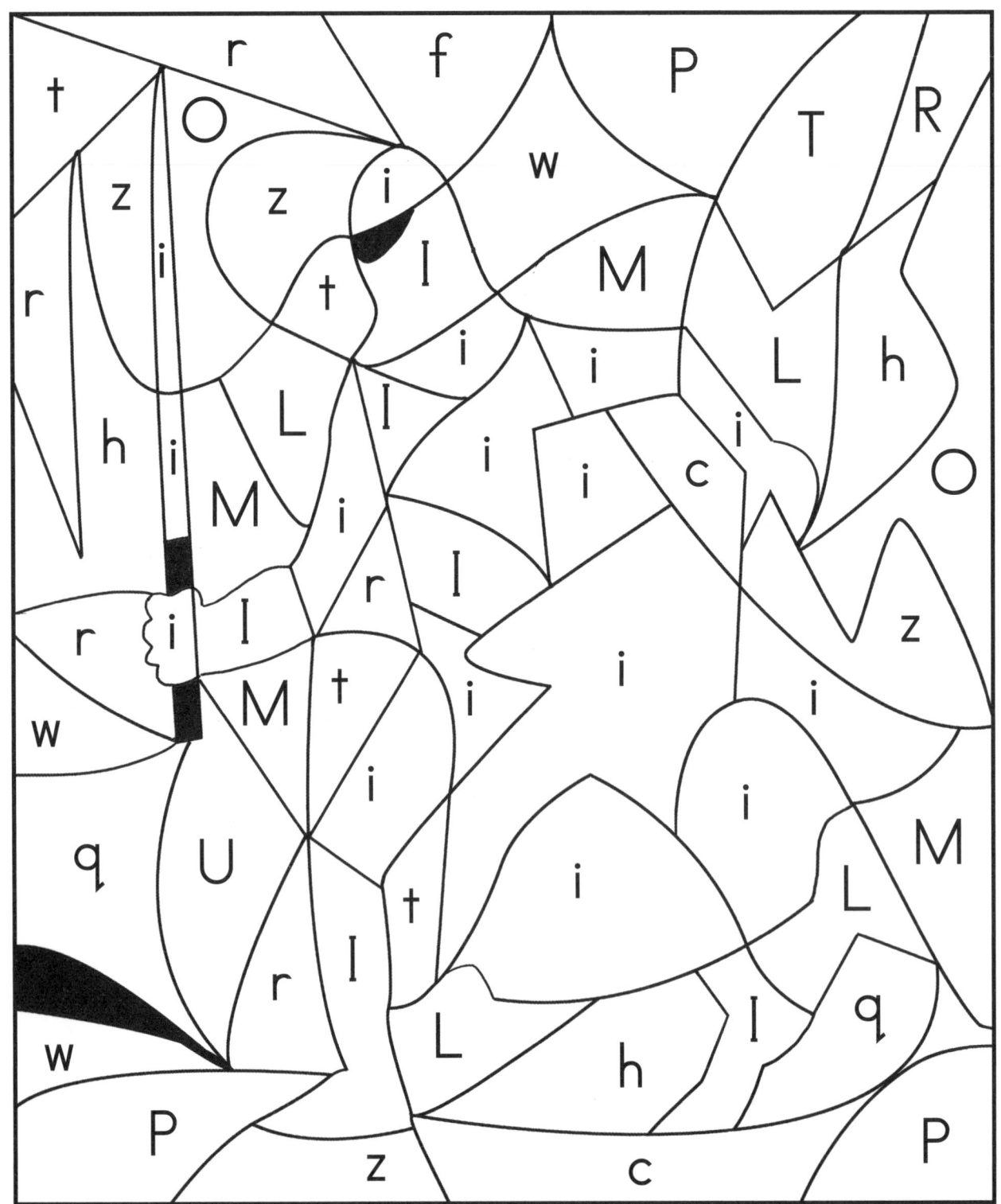

# Play with J

Colour the spaces with **J** in brown.

Colour the spaces with **j** in orange.

Who do you see?

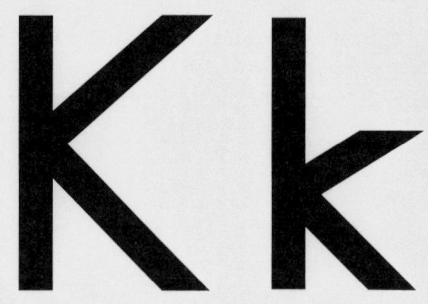
# Kk

Obi-Wan Kenobi keeps the krayt dragon from attacking the Jedi.

Copy the capital letter **K**.

Now write the capital letter **K**.

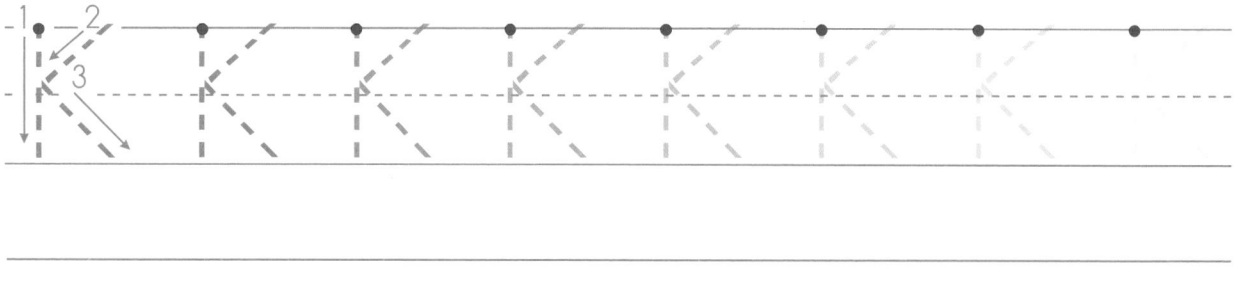

Copy the lowercase letter **k**.

Now write the lowercase letter **k**.

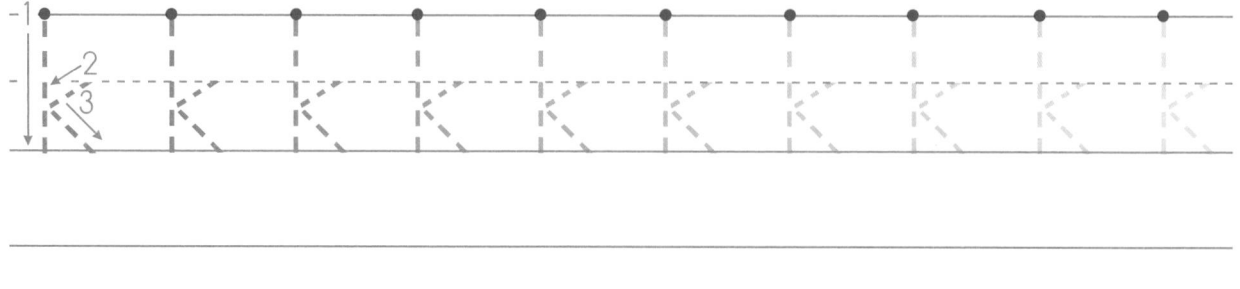

Read the words together.

Now copy the letter **K** or **k** to complete each word.

Plo Koon    Kit Fisto

krayt    kiss    keep

Ki-Adi-Mundi

# L l

Luke learns to use his lightsaber.

Copy the capital letter **L**.

Now write the capital letter **L**.

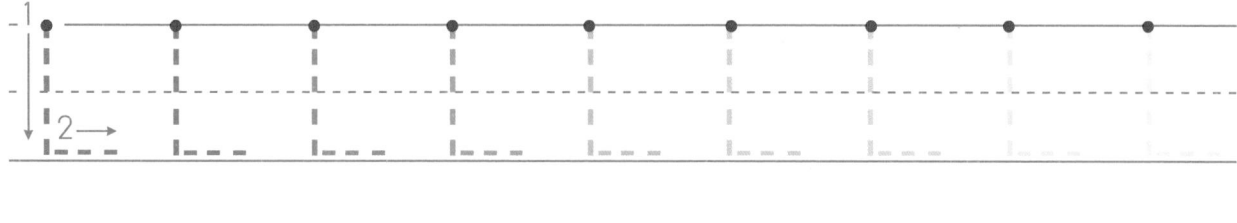

Copy the lowercase letter **l**.

Now write the lowercase letter **l**.

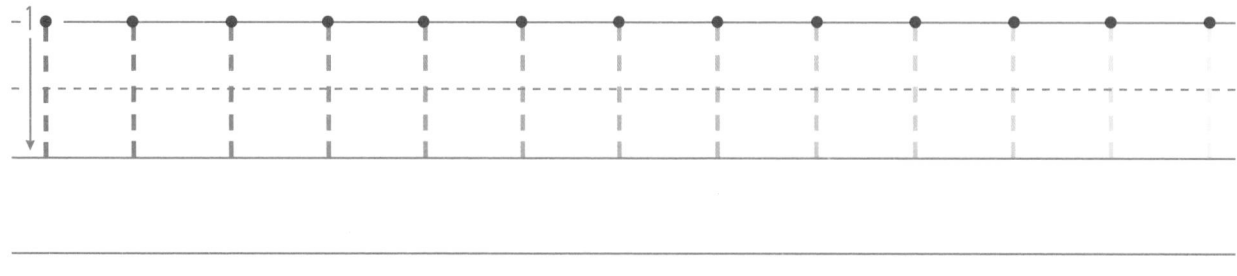

Read the words together.

Now copy the letter L or l to complete each word.

uke

ightsaber

eia

earn

obot

fo ow

# Play with K

Help **Kit** Fisto and Plo **Koon** find **Ki**-Adi-Mundi!

Draw a line along the path with **K** and **k**.

End

k
K

kKKkKKkKkKk
k
K
k

h i f S
J
b
D e p R W h x a j n    KkKKkkKKkKKkkK
A
X
l                                              k
                                                K
i c B j f z H X v y u          k
            t                                   K
            C                                   k
                                                K
kKKkkKKkKkK
k
K                      kKKkkKKkKkkkK
k
K
kkKkKkKkkKK ← Start

# Play with L

Help **Luke** Skywalker through the maze to find his **lightsaber**!

# Mace Windu finds monsters on Mustafar!

Copy the capital letter **M**.

Now write the capital letter **M**.

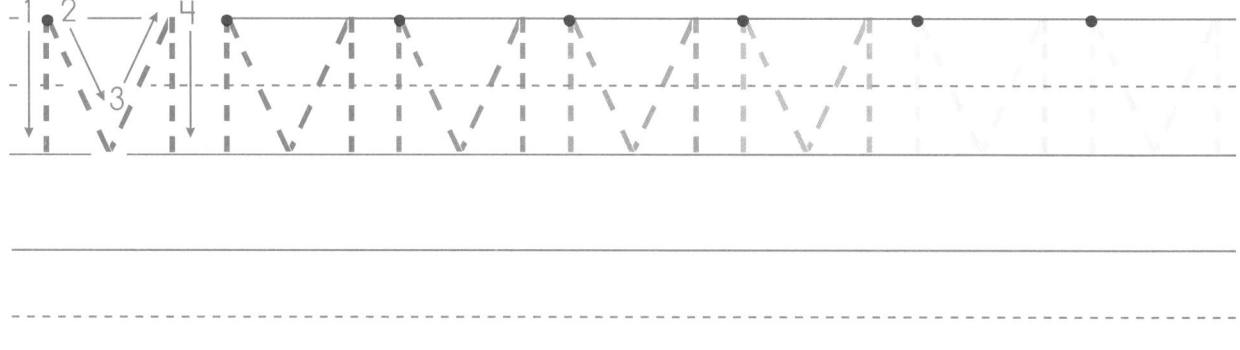

Copy the lowercase letter **m**.

Now write the lowercase letter **m**.

Read the words together.

Now copy the letter **M** or **m** to complete each word.

Mace Windu    smile

Mustafar    monster

Mos Eisley    moon

# N n

Nute Gunray needs to get away from the nexu now!

Copy the capital letter **N**.

Now write the capital letter **N**.

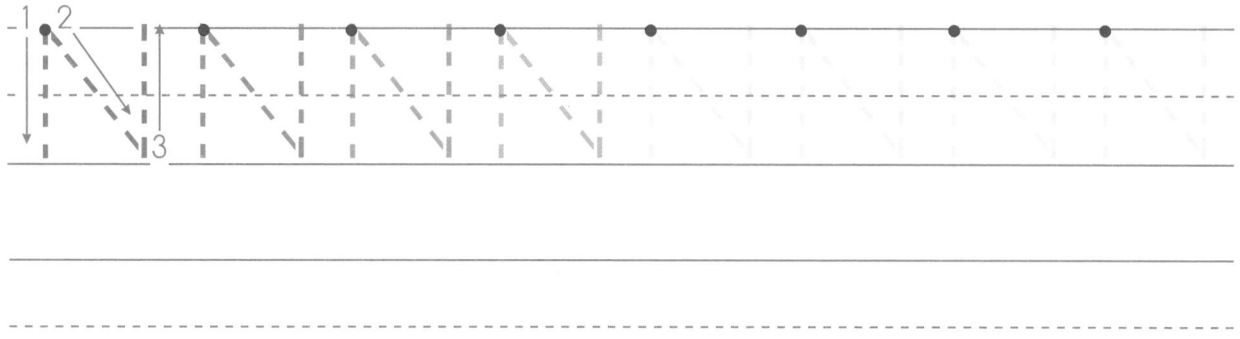

Copy the lowercase letter **n**.

Now write the lowercase letter **n**.

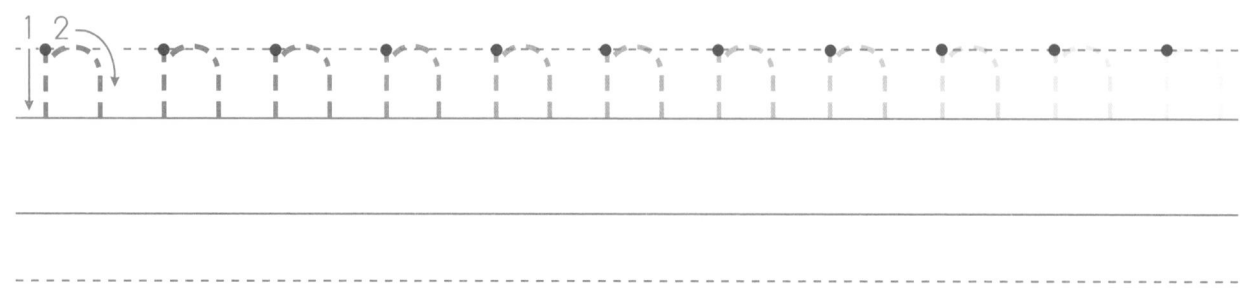

Read the words together.

Now copy the letter **N** or **n** to complete each word.

Nute Gunray now

Naboo tauntaun

nexu Nien Nunb

# Play with M

Colour the moons with **M** and **m** in blue.

# Play with N

Help **Nute** Gunray get away from the **nexu**!

Draw a line along the path with **N** and **n**.

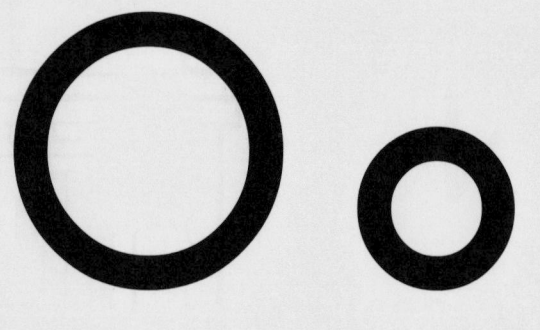

# Oo

The Jedi observes the rocket blast off to Otoh Gunga!

Copy the capital letter O.

Now write the capital letter O.

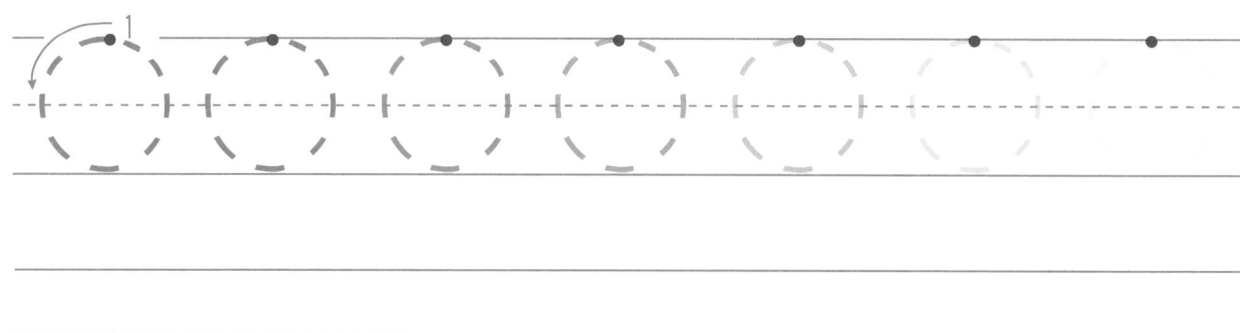

Copy the lowercase letter o.

Now write the lowercase letter o.

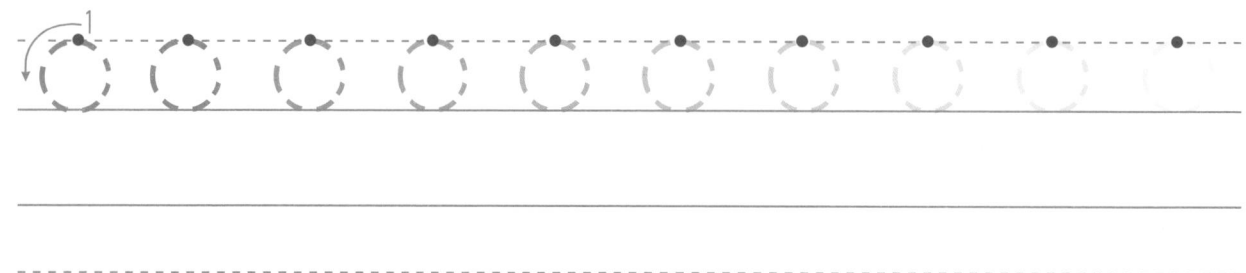

Read the words together.

Now copy the letter O or o to complete each word.

long          observe

rocket        off

otoh Gunga    not

# P p

Padmé flies a purple podracer over the planet.

Copy the capital letter **P**.

Now write the capital letter **P**.

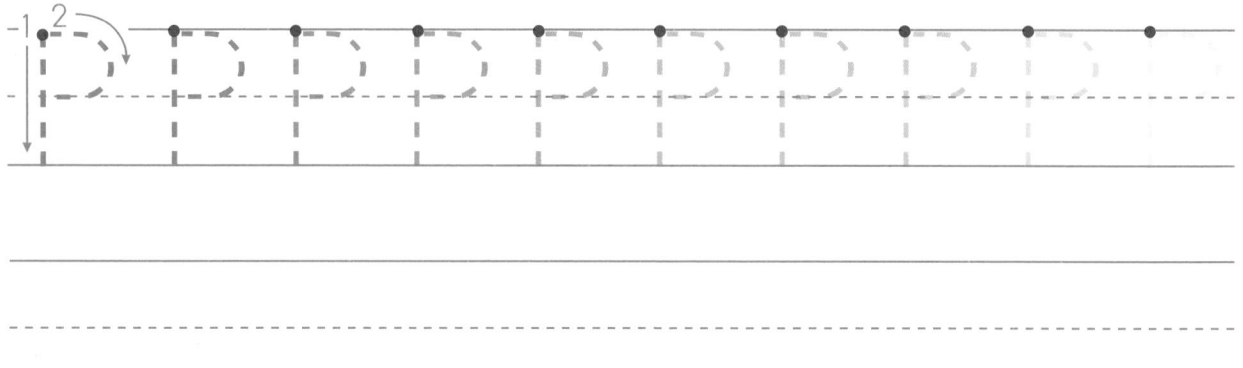

Copy the lowercase letter **p**.

Now write the lowercase letter **p**.

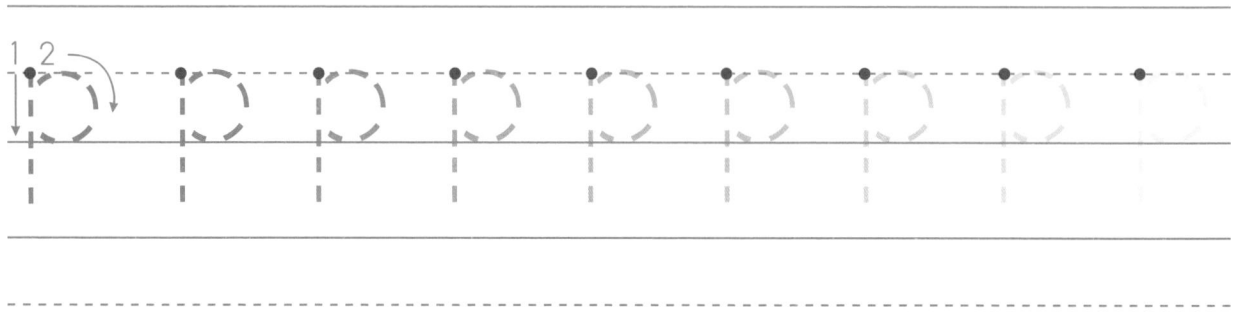

Read the words together.

Now copy the letter **P** or **p** to complete each word.

Padmé    planet

Princess Leia   stop

Plo Koon   podracer

# Play with O

Colour the spaces with **O** in pink.

Colour the spaces with **o** in brown.

Who do you see?

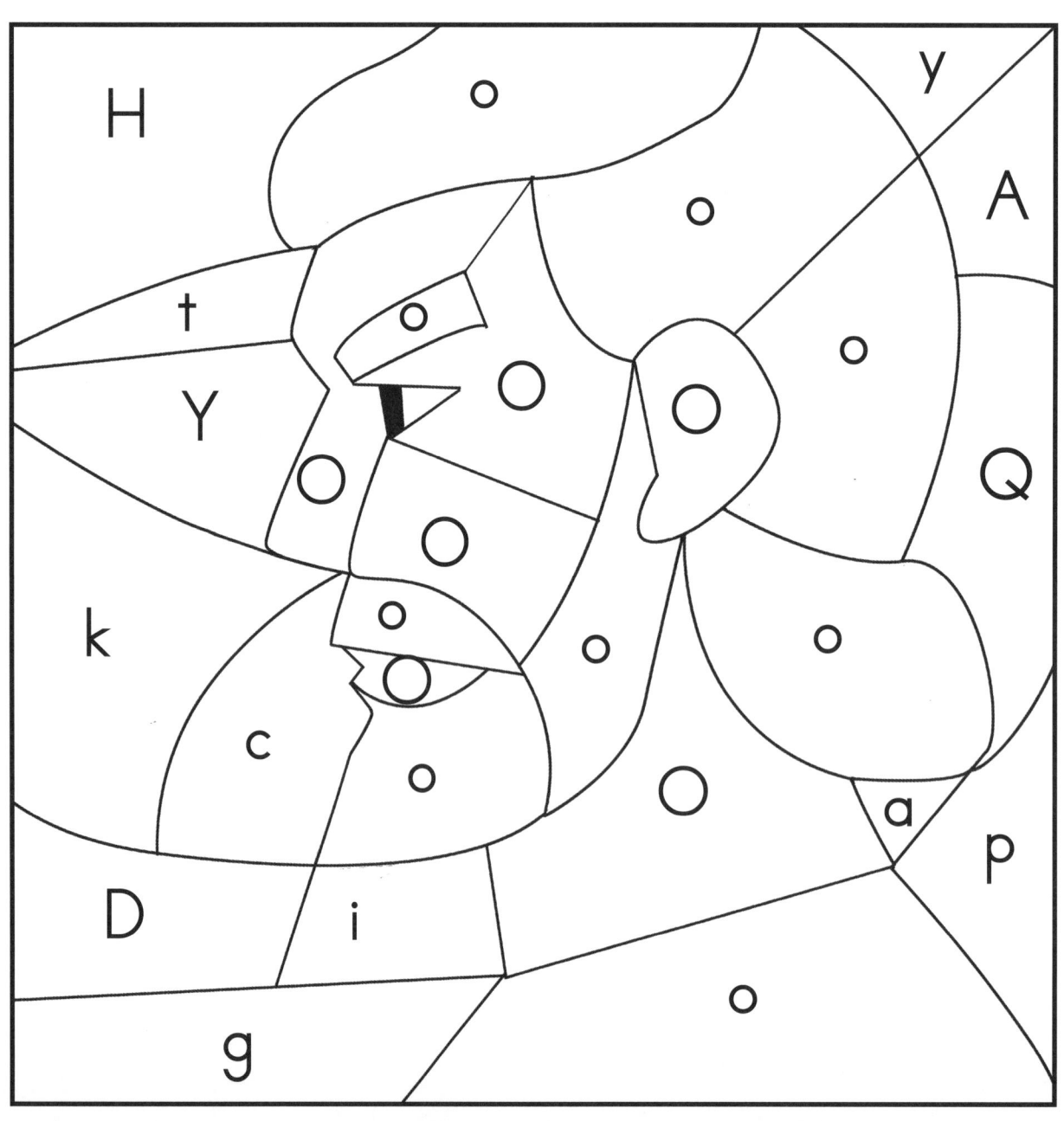

# Play with P

Look at the **podracers**!

Colour in the **podracers** with **P** or **p**.

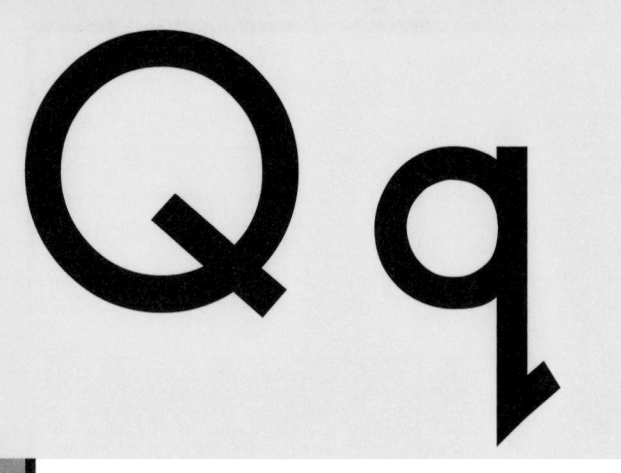

# Q q

Queen Amidala and Qui-Gon Jinn sneak quietly past the guards.

Copy the capital letter **Q**.

Now write the capital letter **Q**.

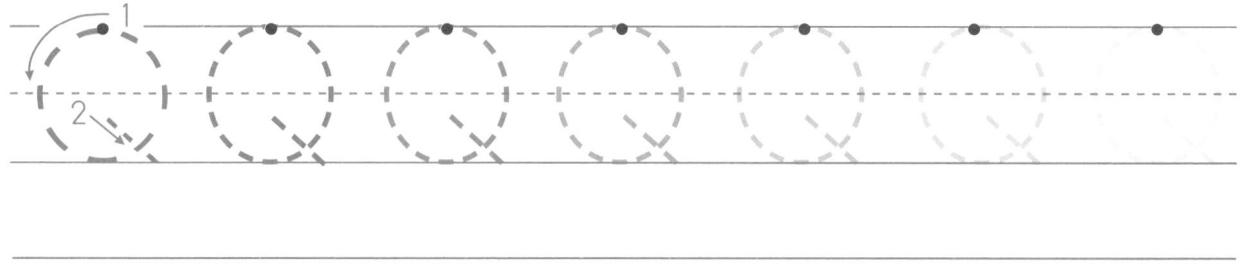

Copy the lowercase letter **q**.

Now write the lowercase letter **q**.

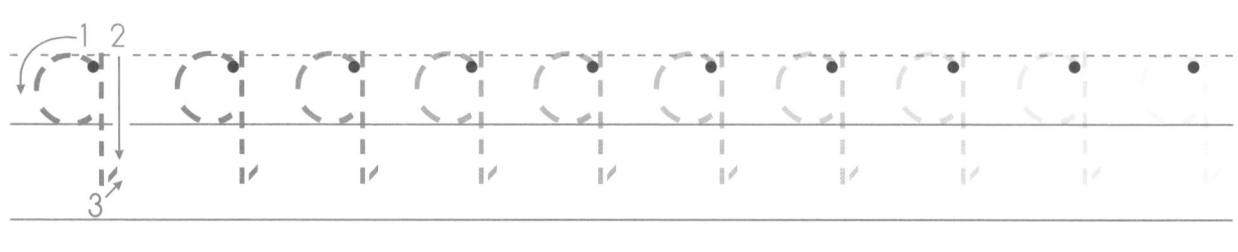

Read the words together.

Now copy the letter **Q** or **q** to complete each word.

Queen  quiet

Qui-Gon Jinn

quiz  quick  equal

# R r

Captain Rex runs ahead of the rancor.

Copy the capital letter **R**.

Now write the capital letter **R**.

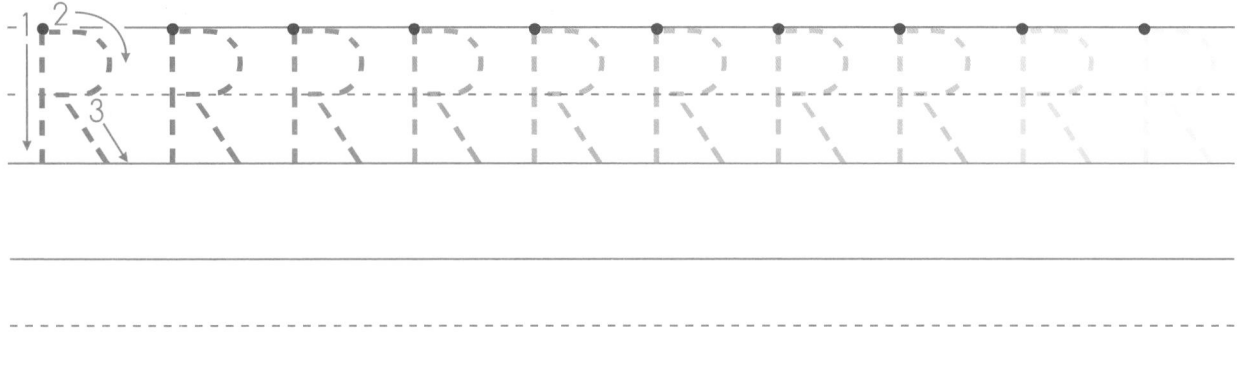

Copy the lowercase letter **r**.

Now write the lowercase letter **r**.

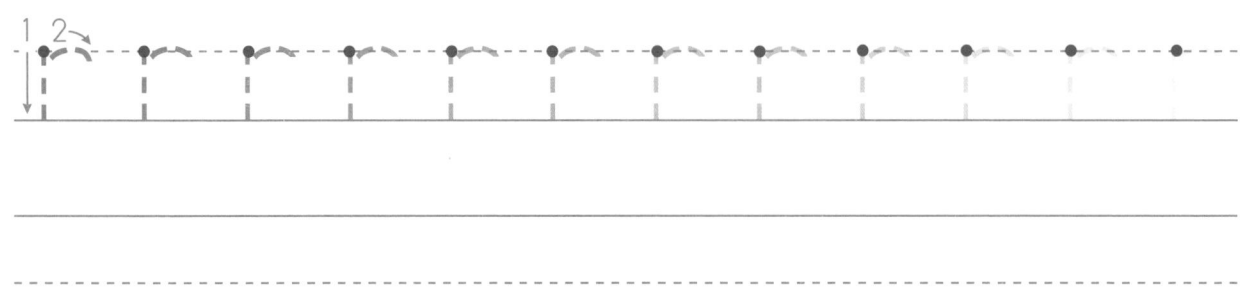

Read the words together.

Now copy the letter **R** or **r** to complete each word.

Captain Rex      run

Republic      rancor

rebel      reek

# Play with Q

Help **Queen** Amidala find **Qui-Gon** Jinn!

Draw a line along the path with **Q** and **q**.

Start → Q q q Q q Y g N u f q x T

# Play with R

Colour the spaces with **R** in blue.

Colour the spaces with **r** in black.

Who do you see?

# S s

Aayla Secura sits
as she sings a song.

Copy the capital letter **S**.

Now write the capital letter **S**.

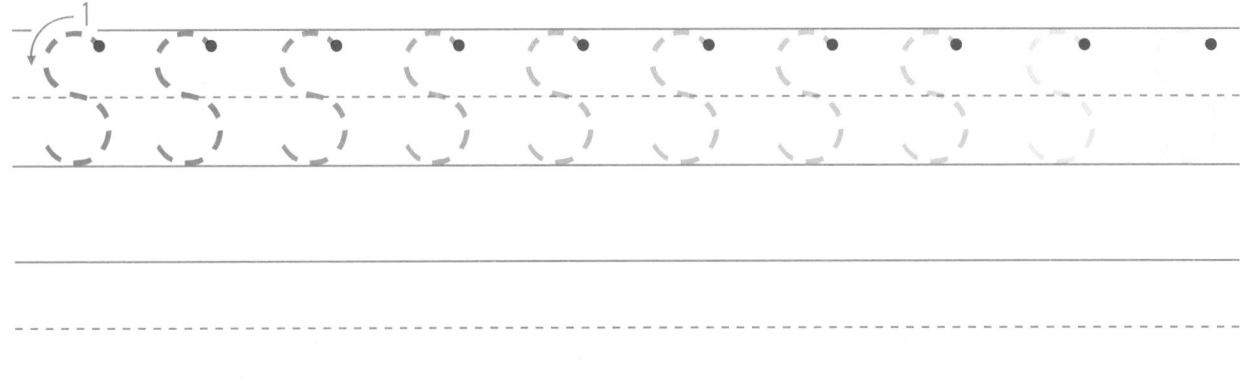

Copy the lowercase letter **s**.

Now write the lowercase letter **s**.

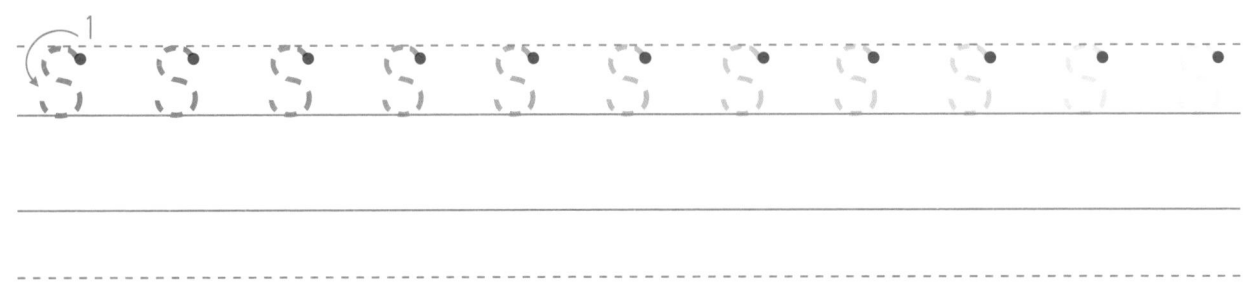

Read the words together.

Now copy the letter **S** or **s** to complete each word.

Sebulba    Sidious

stormtrooper

Secura    Sarlacc

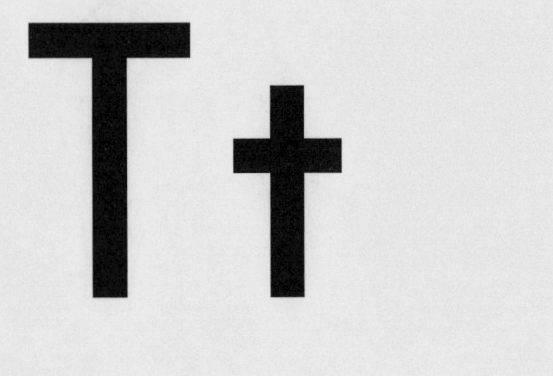

The Tusken Raider travels across Tatooine to his tent!

Copy the capital letter **T**.

Now write the capital letter **T**.

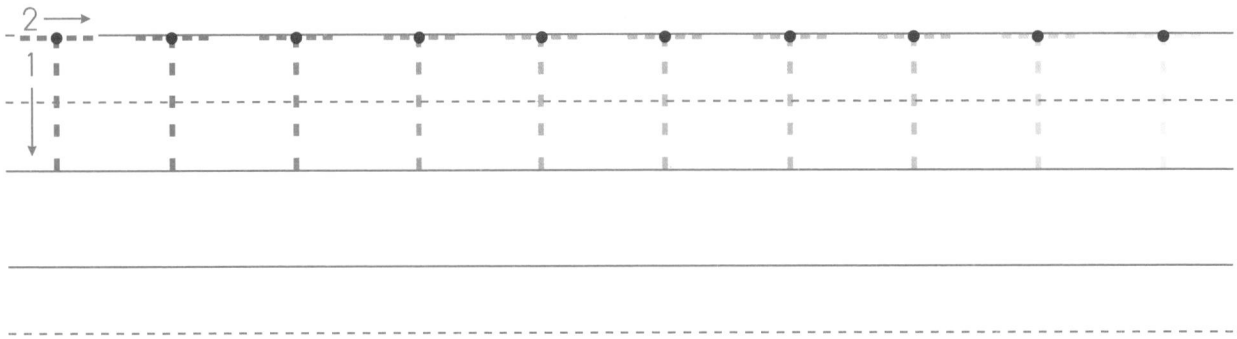

Copy the lowercase letter **t**.

Now write the lowercase letter **t**.

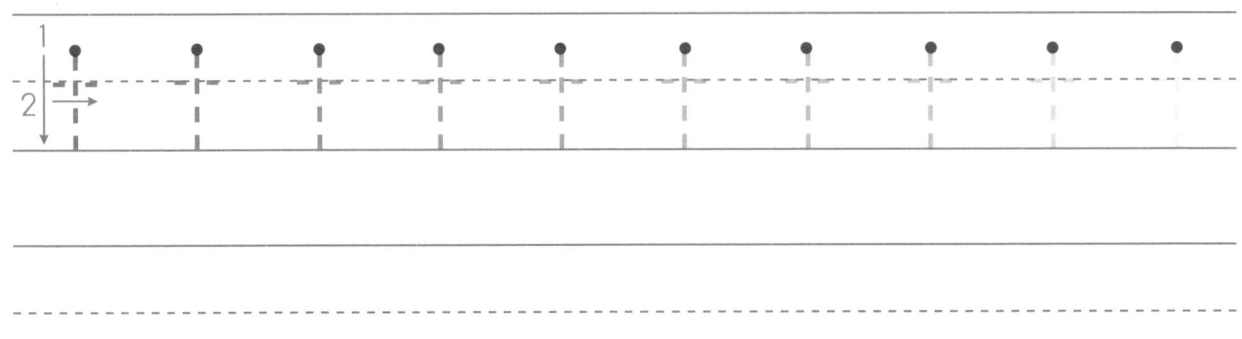

Read the words together.

Now copy the letter T or t to complete each word.

Tusken Raider

Tatooine travel

Twi'lek tent Hutt

# Play with S

What does Aayla Secura see in the doorway?

Colour the spaces with S in blue.

Colour the spaces with s in black.

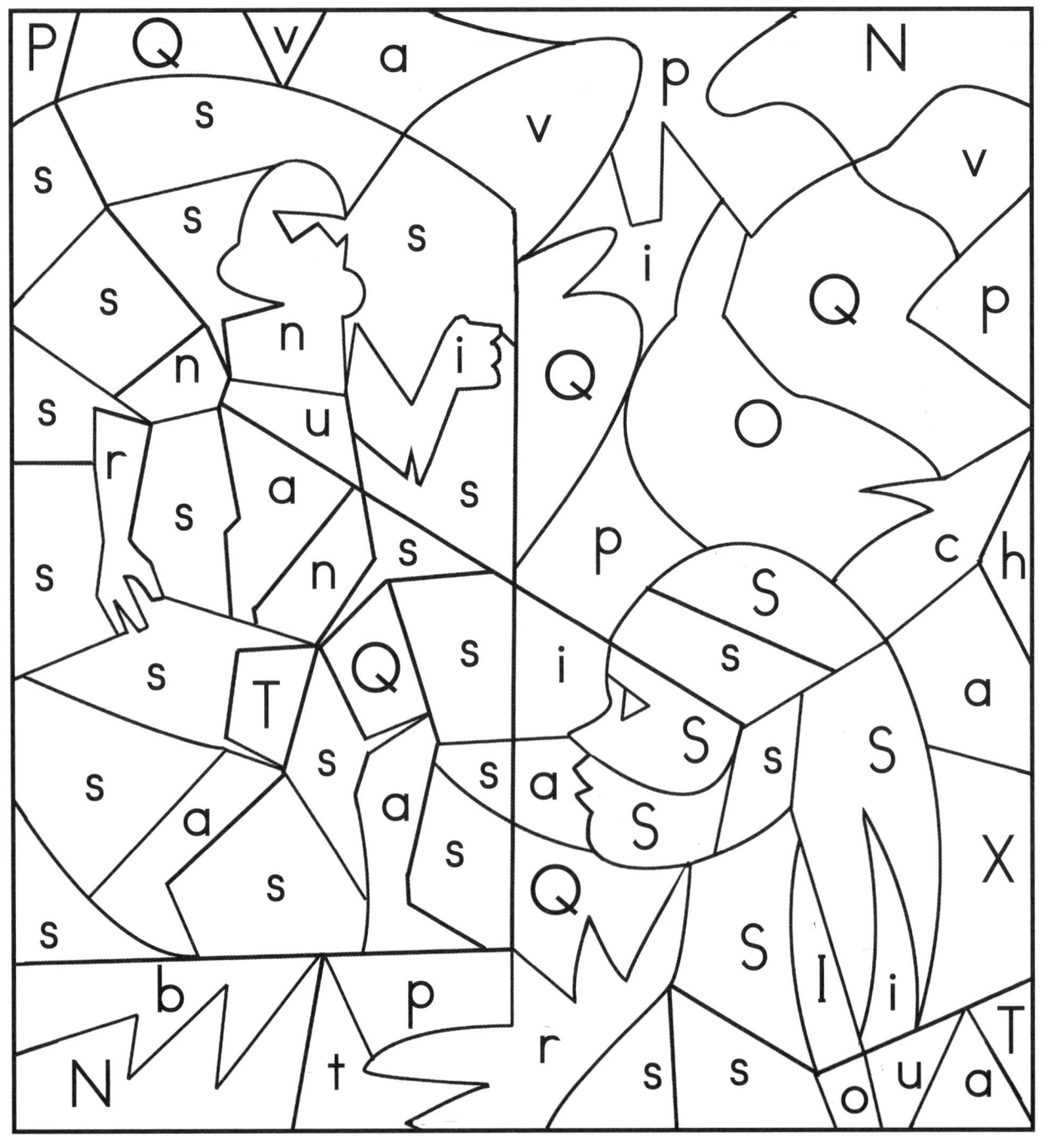

# Play with T

Help the **Tusken** Raider get to his **tent!**

Draw a line along the path with **T** and **t**.

# U u

Luminara Unduli battles Ugnaughts under a tree.

Copy the capital letter **U**.

Now write the capital letter **U**.

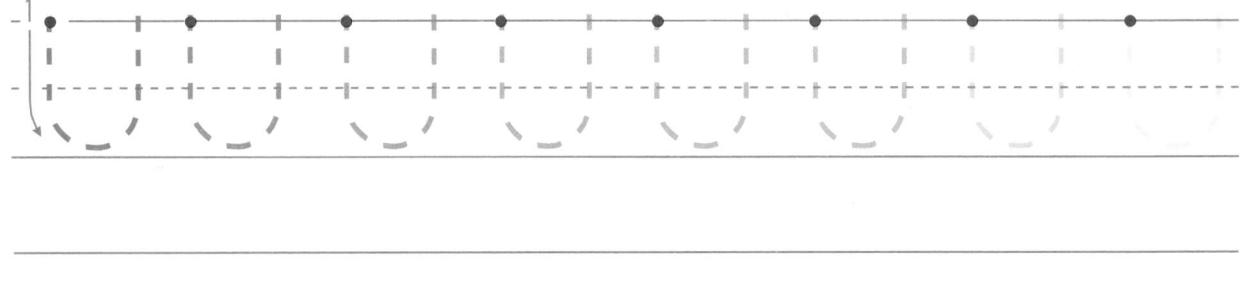

Copy the lowercase letter **u**.

Now write the lowercase letter **u**.

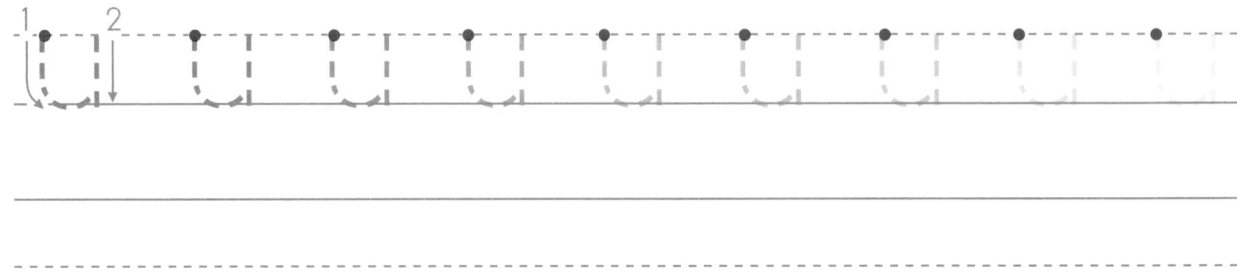

Read the words together.

Now copy the letter **U** or **u** to complete each word.

Luminara Unduli

uncle

under

Ugnaught

until

# V v

Darth Vader rides a very large varactyl.

Copy the capital letter **V**.

Now write the capital letter **V**.

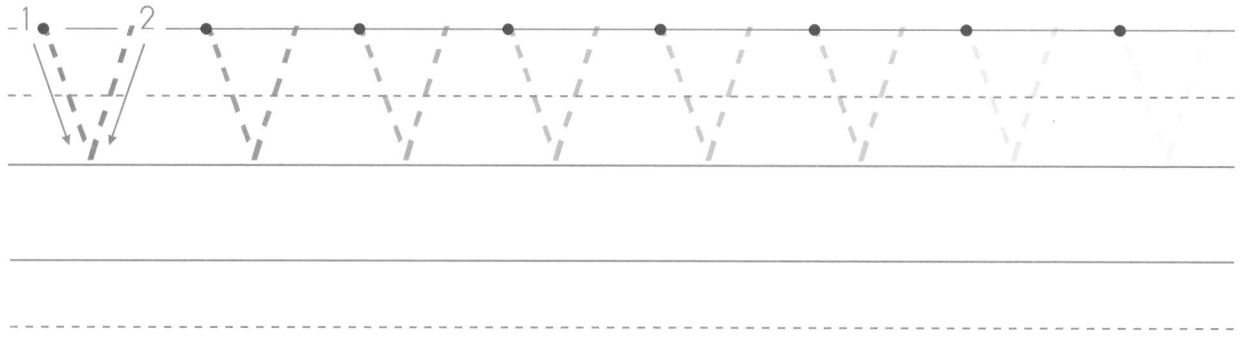

Copy the lowercase letter **v**.

Now write the lowercase letter **v**.

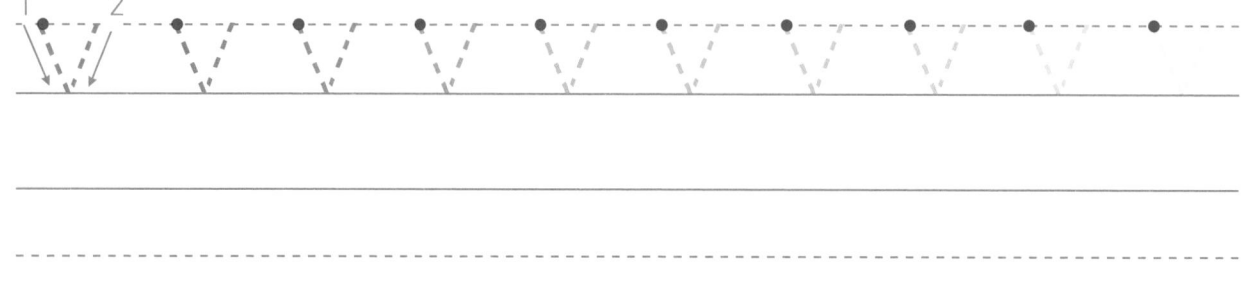

Read the words together.

Now copy the letter V or v to complete each word.

Darth Vader    very

Quinlan Vos

varactyl    even

# Play with U

Help **Luminara Unduli** find the **Ugnaughts**.

Draw a line along the path with **U** and **u**.

# Play with V

Colour the spaces with V in black.

Colour the spaces with v in grey.

Who do you see?

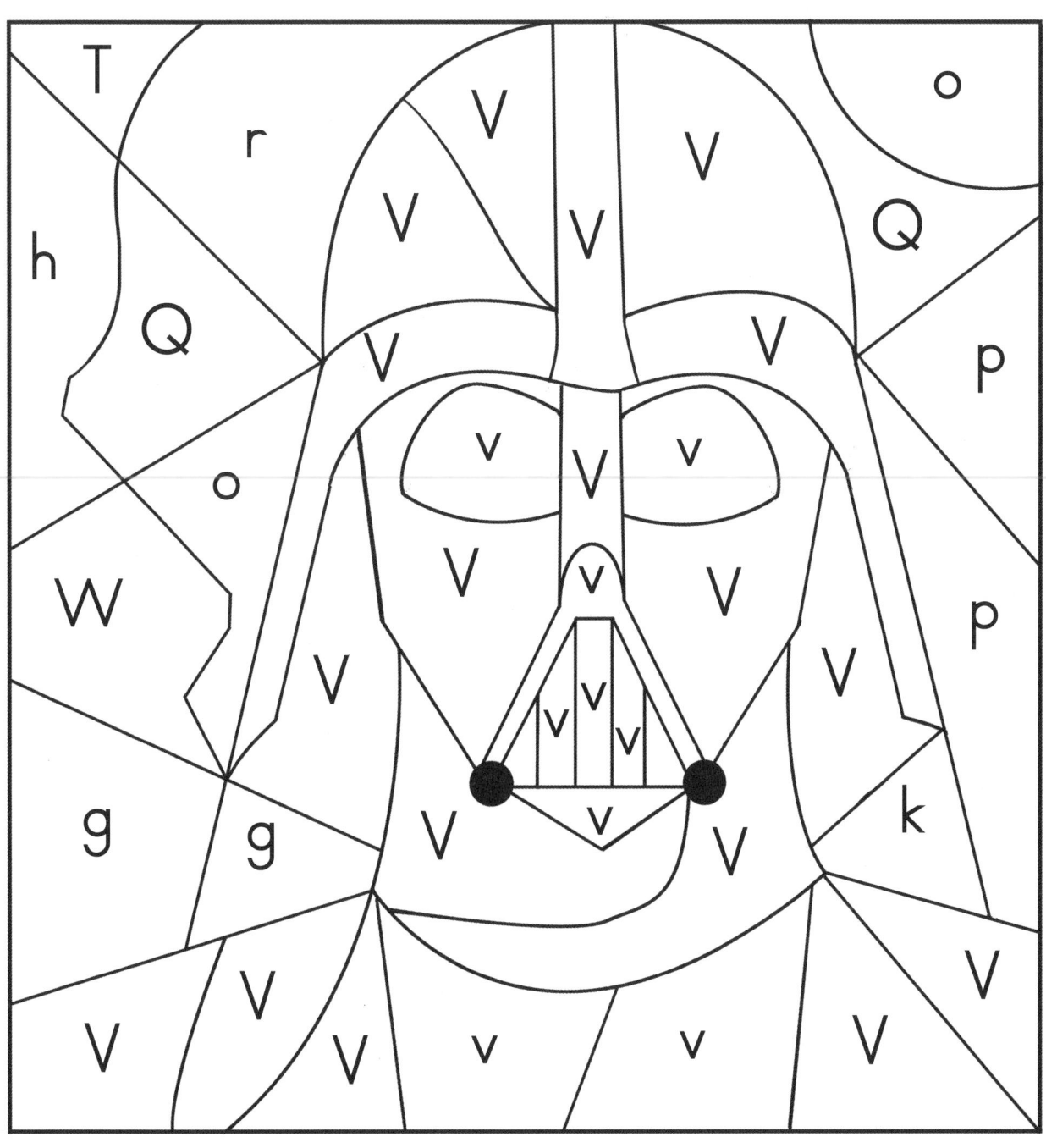

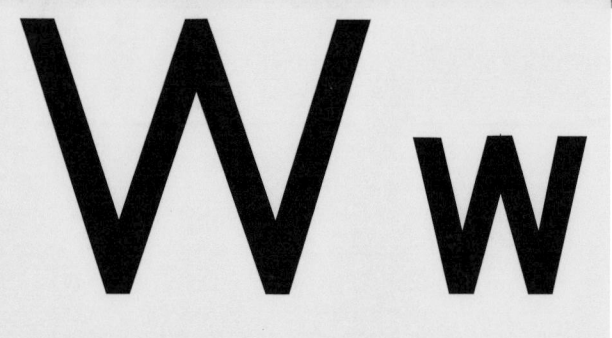

# The Wookiee takes a walk with Wicket the Ewok.

Copy the capital letter **W**.

Now write the capital letter **W**.

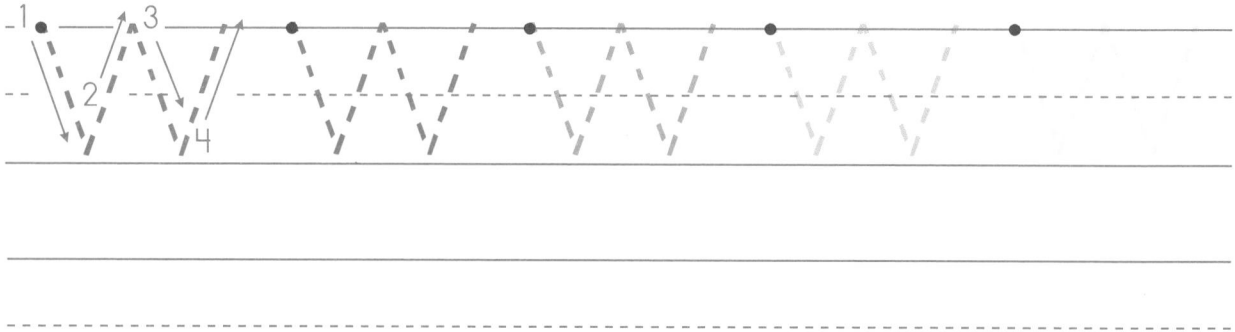

Copy the lowercase letter **w**.

Now write the lowercase letter **w**.

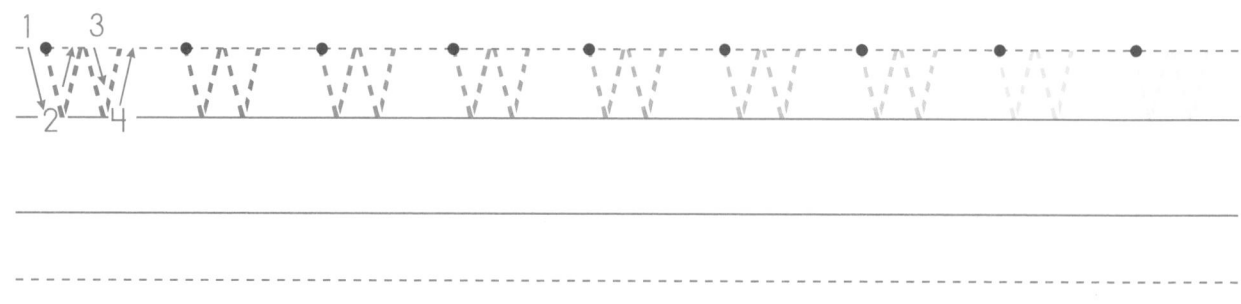

Read the words together.

Now copy the letter **W** or **w** to complete each word.

Wicket     wampa

Ewok     weather

Wookiee     walk

# Xx

The expert pilot flies his X-wing starfighter through the galaxy.

Copy the capital letter **X**.

Now write the capital letter **X**.

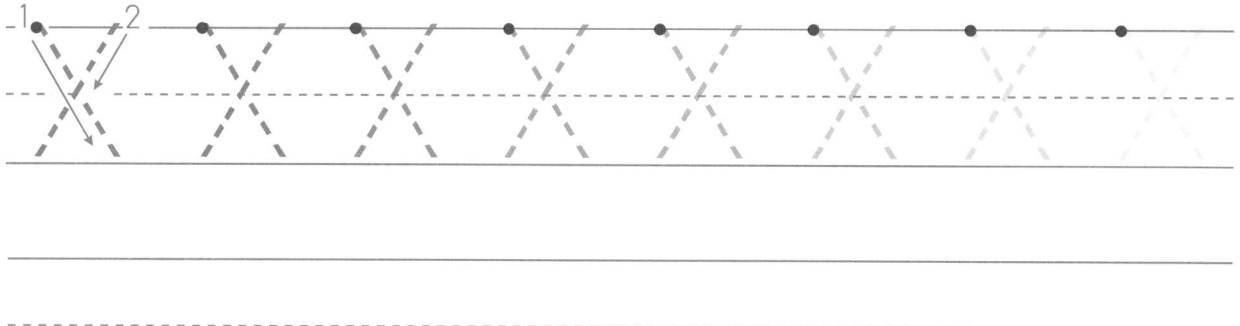

Copy the lowercase letter **x**.

Now write the lowercase letter **x**.

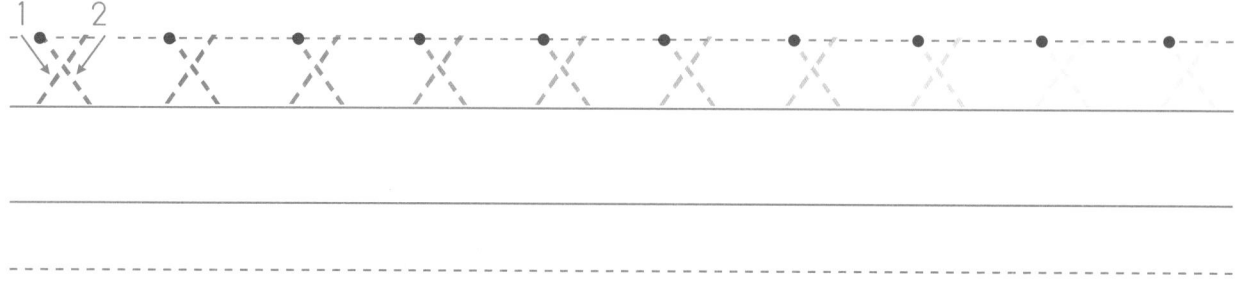

Read the words together.

Now copy the letter **X** or **x** to complete each word.

X-wing

galaxy

X-ray

expert

excellent

exit

# Play with W

Colour the spaces with **W** in brown.

Colour the spaces with **w** in black.

Who do you see?

# Play with X

Help the **X-wing** fighter find the Death Star.

Draw a line along the path with **X** and **x**.

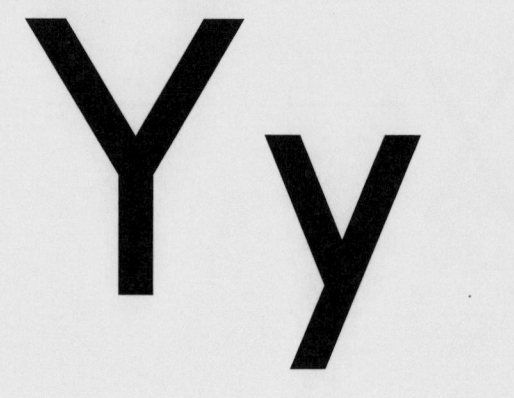

Yoda teaches the younglings about the ways of the Force!

Copy the capital letter **Y**.

Now write the capital letter **Y**.

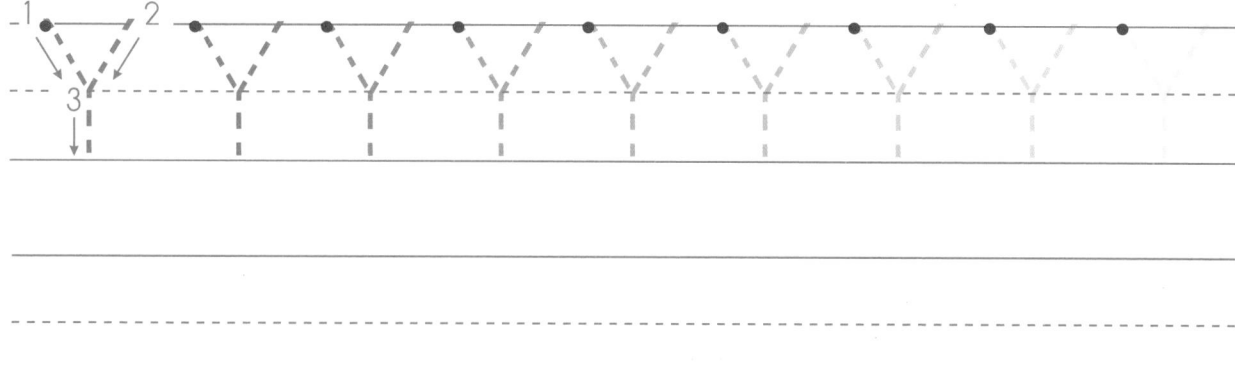

Copy the lowercase letter **y**.

Now write the lowercase letter **y**.

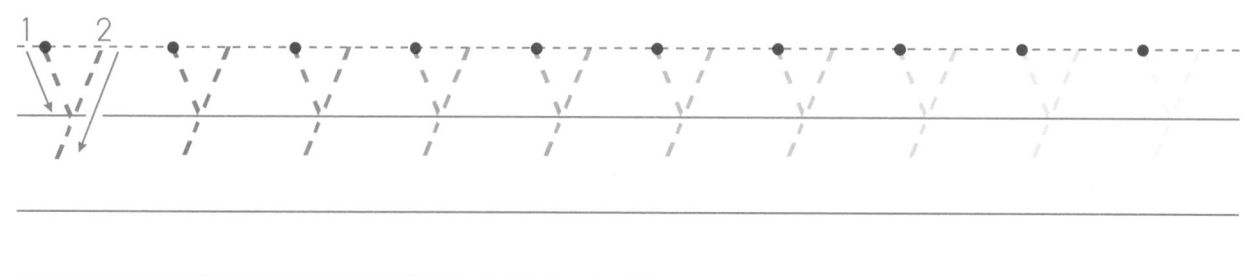

Read the words together.

Now copy the letter Y or y to complete each word.

Yoda     youngling

Yavin    yellow

Yuzzum   yes

# Zz

Zam Wesell zooms through the sky on her home planet, Zolan.

Copy the capital letter **Z**.

Now write the capital letter **Z**.

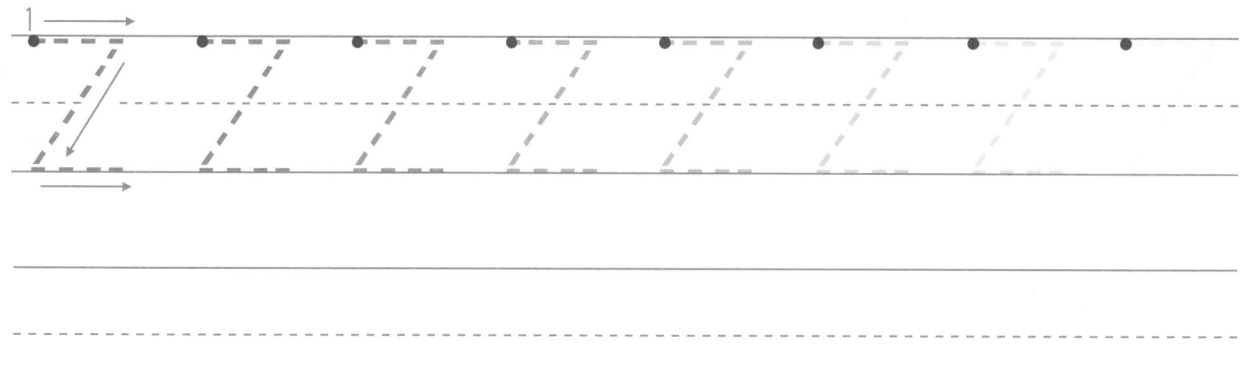

Copy the lowercase letter **z**.

Now write the lowercase letter **z**.

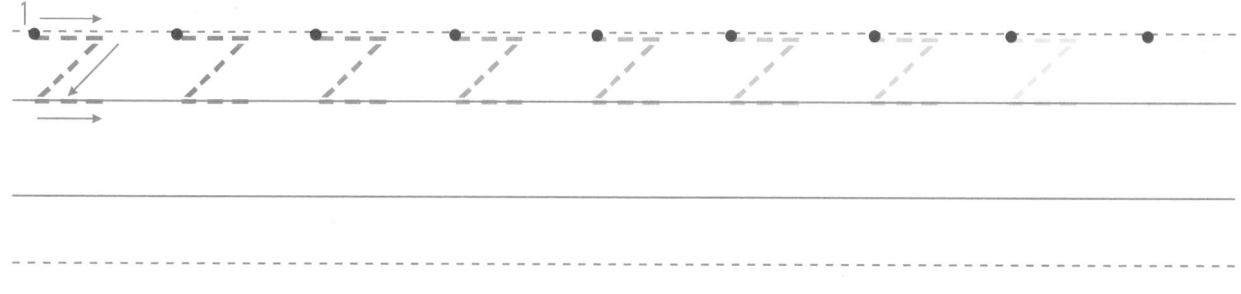

Read the words together.

Now copy the letter **Z** or **z** to complete each word.

Zam

zero

Zolan

zipper

Zuckuss

lazy

# Play with Y

Colour the spaces with **Y** in green.

Colour the spaces with **y** in brown.

Who do you see?

# Play with Z

Help **Zam zigzag** through the maze to find Jango Fett!

End

Start

# Who is this?

Fill in the missing letter to complete his name.

___ o d a

Write his name on the line below.

# Who is this?

Fill in the missing letter to complete his name.

_nakin

Skywalker

Write his name on the lines below.

# Who is this?

Fill in the missing letter
to complete his name.

___uke

Skywalker

Write his name on the
lines below.

# Who is this?

Fill in the missing letter
to complete her name.

___rincess

Leia

Write her name on
the lines below.

# Who is this?

Fill in the missing letter to complete her name.

__ueen

Amidala

Write her name on the lines below.

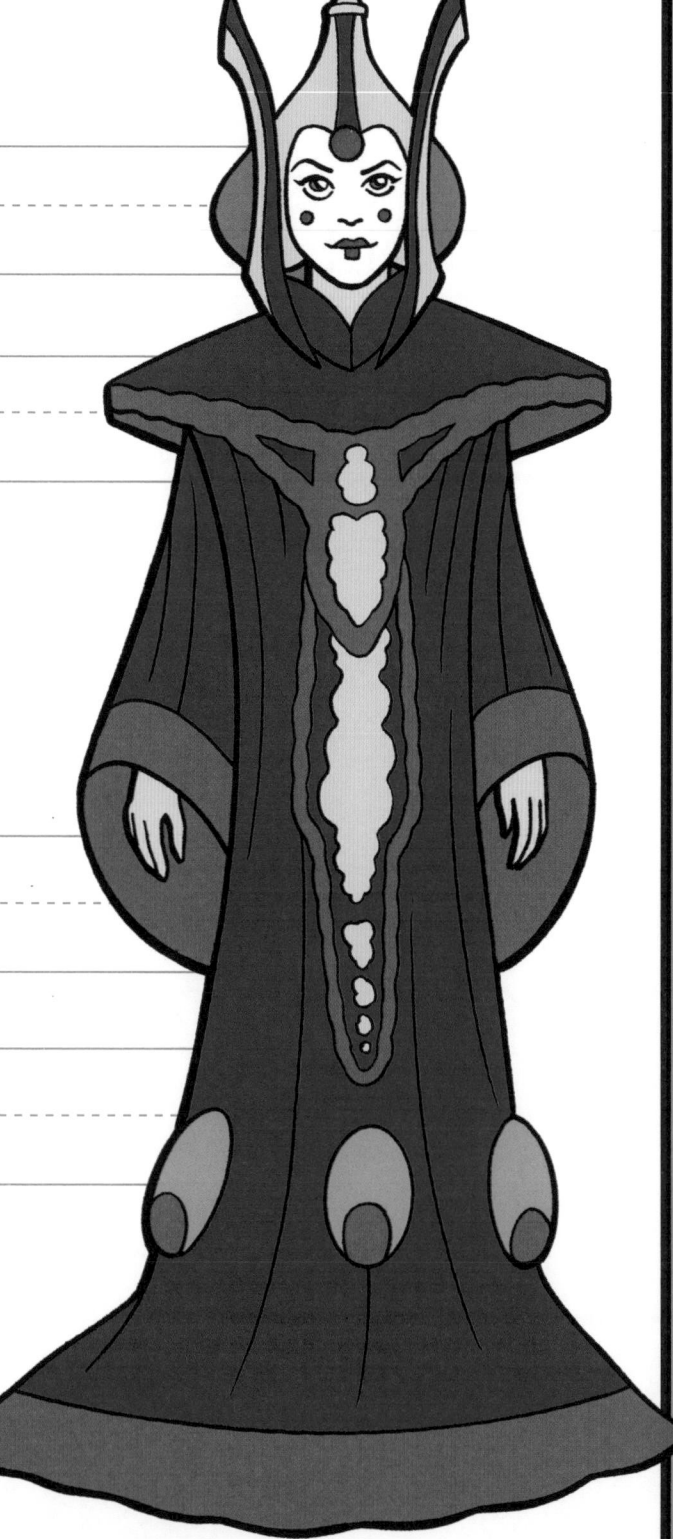

# Who is this?

Fill in the missing letter to complete his name.

Jar Jar

_inks

Write his name on
the lines below.

# Who is this?

Fill in the missing letter to complete his name.

Chewbacc____

Write his name on the line below.

_____

- - - - - - - - - - - - - - - - -

_____

# Who is this?

Fill in the missing letter to complete his name.

Han
Sol_

Write his name on the lines below.

# Who is this?

Fill in the missing letter to complete his name.

## Obi-Wan
## enobi

Write his name on the
lines below.

_____

- - - - - - - - - - -

_____

- - - - - - - - - - -

_____

# Who is this?

Fill in the missing letter to complete his name.

Darth

\_ader

Write his name on the lines below.

# Who is this?

Fill in the missing letter to complete his name.

_arth

Maul

Write his name on the
lines below.

# Who is this?

Fill in the missing letter to complete his name.

Bo␣␣a

Fett

Write his name on the
lines below.

# Answers

pages 8-9
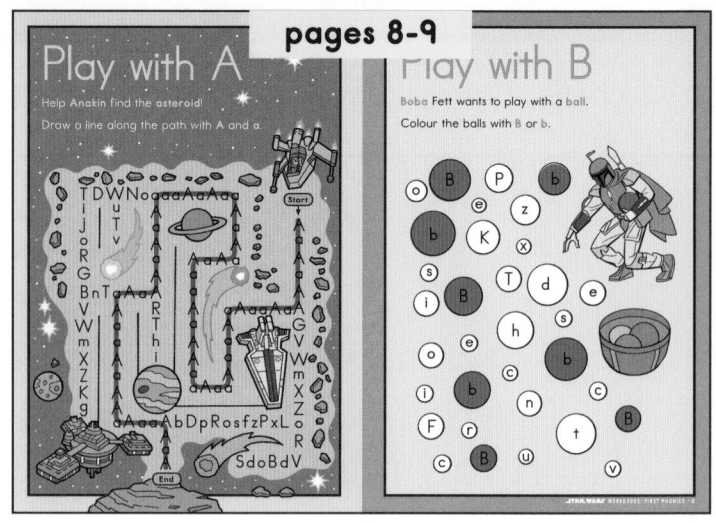

pages 14-15

pages 20-21
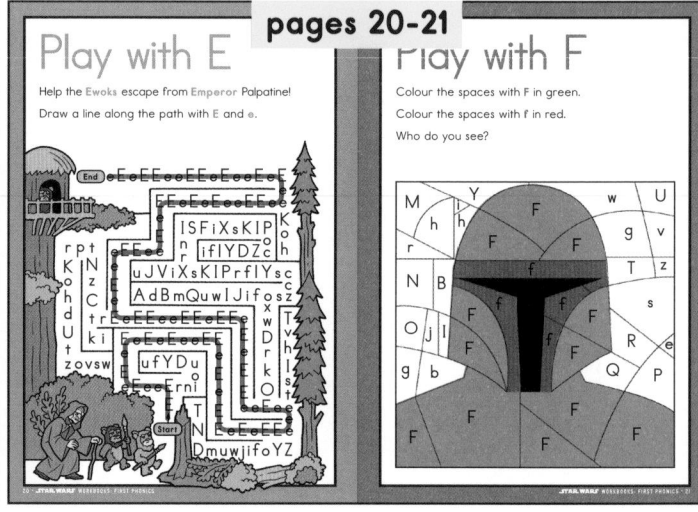

pages 26-27

pages 32-33

pages 38-39

pages 44-45

Play with O
Colour the spaces with O in pink.
Colour the spaces with o in brown.
Who do you see?

Play with P
Look at the podracers!
Colour in the podracers with P or p.

Play with Q
Help Queen Amidala find Qui-Gon Jinn!
Draw a line along the path with Q and q.

Play with R
Colour the spaces with R in blue.
Colour the spaces with r in black.
Who do you see?

Play with S
What does Aayla Secura see in the doorway?
Colour the spaces with S in blue.
Colour the spaces with s in black.

Play with T
Help the Tusken Raider get to his tent!
Draw a line along the path with T and t.

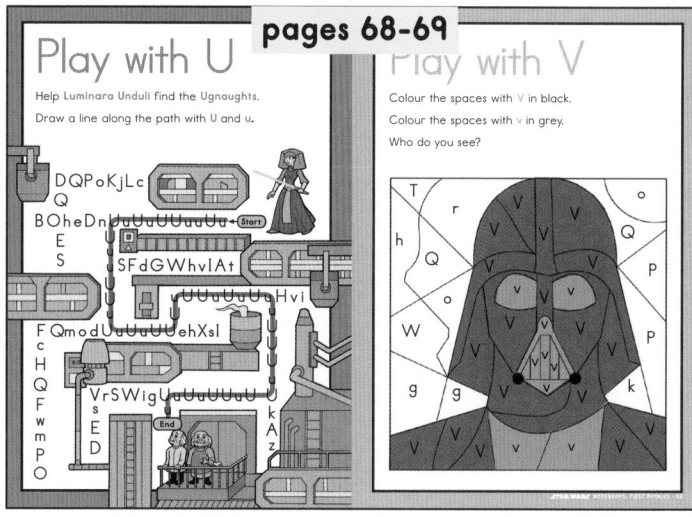

Play with U
Help Luminara Unduli find the Ugnaughts.
Draw a line along the path with U and u.

Play with V
Colour the spaces with V in black.
Colour the spaces with v in grey.
Who do you see?

Play with W
Colour the spaces with W in brown.
Colour the spaces with w in black.
Who do you see?

Play with X
Help the X-wing fighter find the Death Star.
Draw a line along the path with X and x.

Play with Y
Colour the spaces with Y in green.
Colour the spaces with y in brown.
Who do you see?

Play with Z
Help Zam zigzag through the maze to find Jango Fett!

Who is this?
Fill in the missing letter to complete his name.

Yoda

Write his name on the line below.

Yoda

Who is this?
Fill in the missing letter to complete his name.

Anakin Skywalker

Write his name on the lines below.

Anakin Skywalker

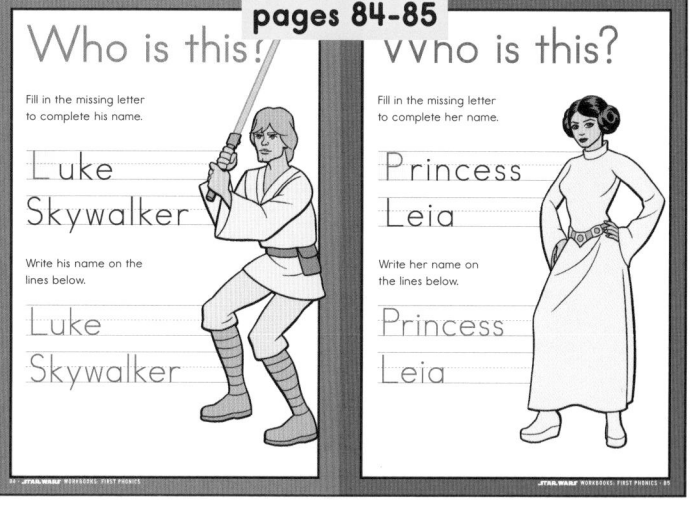

Who is this?
Fill in the missing letter to complete his name.

Luke Skywalker

Write his name on the lines below.

Luke Skywalker

Who is this?
Fill in the missing letter to complete her name.

Princess Leia

Write her name on the lines below.

Princess Leia

# Answers

pages 86-87

pages 88-89

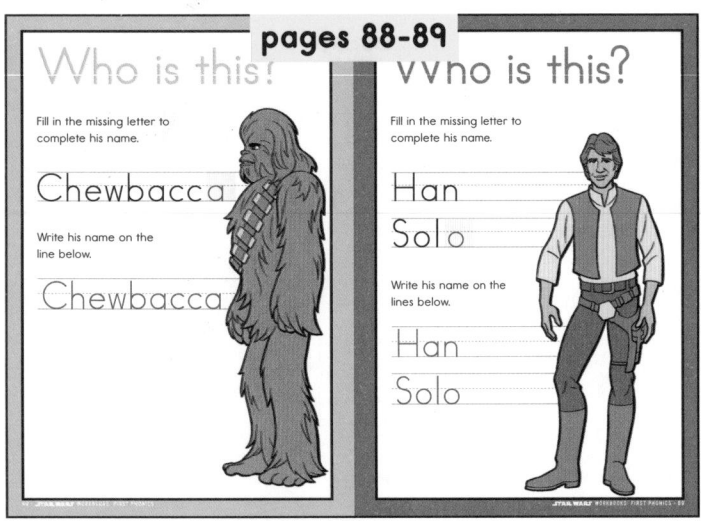

pages 90-91

pages 92-93

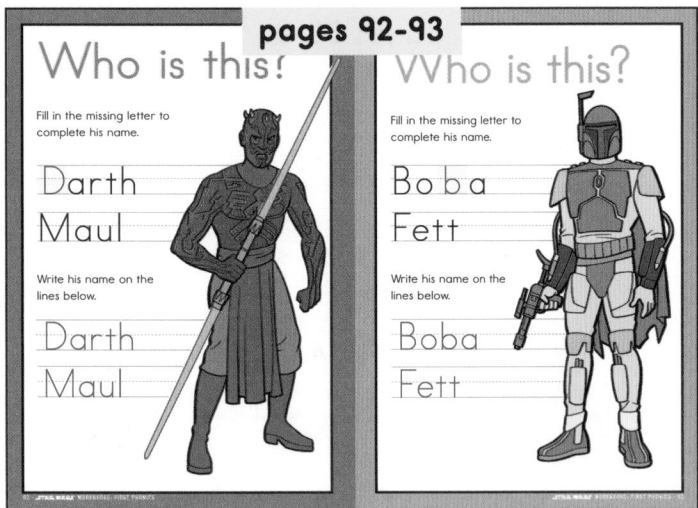